THE ULTIMATE SALES LETTER

Attract New Customers. Boost Your Sales.

Dan S. Kennedy

3rd Edition

BUSINESS

Adams Media
Avon, Massachusetts

Published by Adams Media, an F+W Publications Company
57 Littlefield Street
Avon, MA 02322
www.adamsmedia.com
ISBN 10: 1-59337-499-2
ISBN 13: 978-1-59337-499-0
Printed in the United States of America.

10 9 8 7 6 5 4

Library of Congress Cataloging-in-Publication Data
Kennedy, Dan S.
The ultimate sales letter : attract new customers.
boost your sales / Dan S. Kennedy.—3rd ed.
.   p.   cm.
Includes index.
ISBN 1-59337-499-2
1. Sales letters. 2. Selling. I. Title.
HF5730.K46 2006
658.8'1—dc22

2005026073

The Publisher of this work is in no way responsible for the National Sales Letter Contest
or any other contest affiliated with this book or the author. All contest rules, fulfillment,
liability, and indemnity are the sole responsibility of the author of this work, Dan S. Kennedy.

This publication is designed to provide accurate and authoritative information with regard
to the subject matter covered. It is sold with the understanding that the publisher is not
engaged in rendering legal, accounting, or other professional advice. If legal advice or
other expert assistance is required, the services of a competent professional person should
be sought.
—From a *Declaration of Principles* jointly adopted by a Committee of the
American Bar Association and a Committee of Publishers and Associations

Many of the designations used by manufacturers and sellers to distinguish their products
are claimed as trademarks. Where those designations appear in this book and Adams
Media was aware of a trademark claim, the designations have been printed with initial
capital letters.
Interior design and composition by
Electronic Publishing Services, Inc., Tennessee

This book is available at quantity discounts for bulk purchases.

For information, please call 1-800-289-0963.

Contents

How to Get Maximum Value from This Book

Here are four things you can do to turn this book into an interactive learning experience, to actually write Ultimate Sales Letters you can use, and extend this book into an ongoing business development program.

(1) Throughout the book, you will find little "boxes" headlined RESOURCE! Many of these direct you to Web sites where additional information, expanded examples, and demonstrations of the corresponding strategy discussed in the book can be found. For example, on page 29, we talk about turning Features into Benefits. In the RESOURCE! box, you'll find a Web site where you can get 50 examples of Features converted to Benefits, from actual, successful sales letters.

(2) Enter the National Sales Letter Contest and compete for a brand-new Ford Mustang and other awards! Go to *www.NationalSales LetterContest.com*. By participating in the contest, you'll be motivated to use the strategies presented in this book—to take action! All you need to do now is register. The contest extends for 18 months from the first publication of this book. If you enter during that time period, you'll be eligible to win the Mustang. If the contest has ended by the time you get this book, you'll find a modified "consolation competition" that will award a prize every 90 days.

(3) Enroll in a free 12-Week Ultimate Sales Letter Course delivered by e-mail, at *www.Ultimate-Sales-Letter.com*.

(4) Register for a free three-month subscription to the author's *No B.S. Marketing Letter* at *www.Ultimate-Sales-Letter.com*.

Since its first publication in 1991, this book has inspired and guided tens of thousands of people in diverse businesses and sales activities to create and use "the ultimate sales letter." Here are a few of their comments:

......

"One sales letter campaign developed from your instructions has actually produced so much business for my practice I no longer have marketing needs. I only have trouble handling all the clients!"
Harry Williams
Attorney, Illinois

......

"I first read *The Ultimate Sales Letter* in July, 1991, and I have reviewed my highlighted, underlined, and dog-eared sections dozens of times. I shamelessly and repeatedly use Step 6 and it has added buckets of money to my political fundraising letters. I bought an extra copy for the National Director of the Libertarian Party. He also swears by it."
Michael Cloud
Speeches People Talk About, Nevada

......

"I manage a direct-mail campaign that sends over 750,000 pieces a month to homeowners. Our direct-mail has resulted in a 300% increase in sales and profits."

Doug Hinton
Seacoast Equities, California

......

"I have invested well over $100,000.00 having Dan Kennedy write ads and sales letters for me. Getting an inside look at his method in this book is the bargain of the century."

Rory Fatt
Restaurant Marketing Systems, Inc., Vancouver B.C.

......

"Hundreds of thousands of dollars have been produced every year, for three years, with one sales letter written with Dan's assistance. A second, new one brought in $165,000.00 the first time it was used."

Tracy Tolleson
Tolleson Mortgage Publications, Arizona

......

"Carefully following the instructions in *The Ultimate Sales Letter*, I put together a long letter for the purpose of securing appointments with top decision-makers in my industry. In over 20 years in this business, I've never sent anything longer than a one-page letter, and frankly, I doubted your approach. But this time, instead of fighting through secretaries and making follow-up call after follow-up call, these prospects were calling me. So far, I've written over $50,000.00 in new business from mailing only 2,500 letters."

John Cummings
Michigan

......

"Could direct-mail work for a little store like ours? Following *The Ultimate Sales Letter*, we sent out a 4-page letter to all the people in our area, followed by three postcards, and we brought in over 100 new customers, and immediately got back our little investment ten times over."

Mary and Walter Bruchan
Washington

......

"I've been a marketing director for nearly ten years. I know quite a bit. My promotions pulled results, bosses and clients loved me. But I was not aware of how much I didn't know! . . . if Dan Kennedy required my next born child in exchange for the information he has given, I'd pay to have a reversal of my tubal ligation."

Bridget Campbell
Idaho

......

And from Down Under . . .

"I have been a keen student of yours for close to ten years. More than any other direct marketing expert on the planet, it is your tactics, strategies and principles that have directly contributed to my success. From a Dan Kennedy neophyte to Kennedy expert, my achievements, including being CEO of Australia's 29th fastest growing company and achieving rank of Australia's 39th richest young entrepreneur (per *Business Review Weekly* Magazine), can be attributed to your teachings. Our products are now in every department store in the U.S., the GNC stores, and we are looking forward to exponential growth this year."

Peter Nichols, CEO
Naturopathica, Skin Doctors Cosmeceuticals
Sydney, Australia

......

"There have been great copywriters in the past 25 years that are without peer. After the death of Eugene Schwarz, there are only three left living and you, Dan Kennedy, are one of the three! Your copywriting advice, like that in *The Ultimate Sales Letter*, has helped me write copy that makes more than $60 million a year. You are my secret weapon."

Sonia Amoroso
Naturopathica, Skin Doctors Cosmeceuticals
Sydney, Australia

SECTION 1

Before You Write a Word . . .

What to Do
Before You Start Writing

I am convinced that just about anybody can learn to craft very effective sales letters. I have no opinion one way or the other about your ability to write the next Great American Novel, a cookbook, a children's storybook, or a Broadway play. (I've written a country-and-western song— "I Love My Wife But I Forgot Where I Live"—but that's another story.) I do, though, have great confidence in your ability to write a successful sales letter, for two basic reasons.

First, you presumably know more about your business, product, service, and customer than anybody else. Writing with that understanding is easy. Getting that understanding is the hard part. When we freelancers are brought in to write sales letters, we have to do our best to acquire that understanding before we can even begin writing. That takes a lot of time and effort and energy, and there's still no way we can get exactly the same full understanding, the same intuitive insights from experience, that you must have in your chosen business. This is a tremendous advantage and you, my friend, possess it.

Second, my own background tells me that just about anybody can learn to do this. I am a high school, not a college, graduate. I did not go to work in the mailroom of some ad agency and learn the trade of copywriting from experienced, seasoned pros while pulling myself up the corporate ladder. In fact, I got my first paid copywriting assignment while still a senior in high school and opened my own ad agency two years later, with no relevant experience or education behind me. I just did the same things you can do:

1. I got books like this one, devoured them, kept them handy, and used them as guides. I sure wish there had been a book exactly like this one, with a step-by-step system, but there were and are plenty of other good ones.
2. I used my own insight, intuition, powers of observation, and common sense.
3. I translated what I knew (and what I kept discovering) about selling and communicating in person to the task of selling and communicating in print.
4. I built up huge "idea files"—samples of ads, mailings, and sales letters. These are called "swipe files" by pros, and that is exactly what they are used for—to swipe ideas from. You do not need much creativity to write letters; you only need to be adept at recycling and reorganizing ideas, themes, words, and phrases.

In spite of my lack of formal education or training in this field, I've developed literally thousands of print ads, sales letters, direct-mail campaigns, and online campaigns for hundreds of clients, and more than 90 percent have been successful. Even though I am paid from $25,000.00 to $75,000.00 plus royalties for such a campaign, more than 85 percent of all clients who use me once do so repeatedly, and some, continuously. Many of my sales letters have been tested against established successes written by other top professional copywriters, and I've won these "beat the best" competitions almost every time. I do not tell you all this to brag; I tell it so that you will realize that you can do it, too. I'm self-taught. You can be self-taught.

Also, for most of your purposes, you do not need the same skill level that I or other top, professional copywriters have painstakingly developed. In most situations I work in, I'm putting together sales letters that will compete against other sales letters written by other top pros, but you will more likely be competing in an environment in which top-flight pro copywriters do not prowl.

I have been motivated—and urge you to be motivated—by what another top copywriter, John Francis Tighe, says frequently: "In the land of the blind, the one-eyed man is king."

Since this book was first published, I've received literally thousands of success stories from people in every imaginable business or sales career who have used this book as their guide, put together a sales letter from scratch, and achieved desirable and profitable results. Some have gone on to great proficiency. Several have become consultants and copywriters.

I recognize that a large part of your success will depend on your being confident that you can write great sales letters. The mechanics are all here for you. But ultimately, you have to go from reading this book to following its steps toward getting sales letters prepared and into the mail.

Here are some general ideas that will help you get started:

1. Don't be intimidated by the idea or process of writing. There's no magic or genius or Harvard degree required.
2. Recognize the value and power of your unique understanding of your business, products, services, and customers. You may find it useful to build reference lists or stacks of 3" × 5" cards—"What I Know About Our Customers . . . About Our Product . . ." and so on.
3. Assemble and organize ideas and samples in a "swipe file"; assemble and organize good reference materials.
4. Think "selling." If you have successful sales experience—terrific! Writing a sales letter is much more akin to getting down on the

living room floor with Ma, Pa, the kids, and the dog and selling a vacuum cleaner than it is to anything else.

If you don't have a "selling mentality," get one! Get some good books about selling. (See my Web site, *www.dankennedy.com*, and this publisher's Web site, *www.adamsmedia.com*, for some ideas.) Never forget that a sales letter is a sales presentation in print.

5. Write. Don't worry about writing a letter from start to finish. Just write blocks of copy and stack them up. A lot of great sales letters are eventually put together with scissors and tape (or by cutting and pasting using a word processing program). Just write!

6. Avoid perfectionism. In most businesses, for most purposes, you don't need a perfect sales letter to get good results. If you follow the guidelines in this book, have something worthwhile to offer, and understand your customer, you may not put together the perfect sales letter, but I'll bet you do put together one that works.

Many people believe that the great, persuasive sales letter writers just sit down at their computers and let the priceless prose flow! I have known two or three who can do this, but most do not. Most professional sales letter writers give themselves the advantage of careful, thorough preparation, and you should, too.

Remember, the more you write, the easier it will get. Just about everything you do easily now was once difficult to do. From fear to confidence; from difficult to easy; from incompetent to competent—that's a movement we repeat over and over again throughout our lives. It's the process that gives life meaning, that prevents boredom, burnout, and depression. It's good for you! It builds healthy self-esteem, which prevents unhealthy addictions and destructive behavior. Gaining new competence in any skill, such as writing sales letters, automatically enhances your confidence in all other areas! In short, you're going to find the ability to craft effective sales letters to be a major asset personally and for your company.

Just as I am convinced that anybody can master the craft of writing effective sales letters, I am also convinced that a sales letter can be developed to sell anything.

One inspiring example of both premises is my Gold/VIP Member Darin Garman. Darin is a former Iowa prison guard turned commercial real estate broker and investor, now a millionaire who deals with millionaire investors. He has successfully attracted clients from all over America to invest, often sight unseen, in Iowa apartment buildings and other properties. His ads appear in national publications such as *Forbes* and *Investors Business Daily*; his letters persuade everyone—kings, oil barons, CEOs, small business owners, and hard-working men and women who are investing to get ahead—to pay a fee just for the right to do business with him. He has written all of his sales letters himself, as a self-taught and otherwise wholly unqualified writer, by following guides including this book. Darin even uses sales letters to sell individual properties. Exhibit #1, a letter plus a response form for one of his properties, appears at the end of this section. It sold out this investment within days of being mailed! There are many lessons to be learned from this terrific sales letter—but the biggest lessons are these:

- Anyone can do it. You can too.
- You can use sales letters to achieve any objective, to sell anything, to promote any business.

Exhibit #1

THIS EXCLUSIVE REPORT IS ONLY INTENDED FOR PERSONS REQUESTING INFORMATION ON THE SHADOWOOD APARTMENTS...

After 'hanging out' with these people for over 10 years I have figured out...

"Why The Shadowood Apartments Is The Kind Of Apartment Property That My Most Successful Apartment Property Investors Put Their Money Into– And How _YOU_ Can Join Them"

For those apartment investors and owners that want to earn as much money in a short period of time there is one thing that has to be present. One thing above all else to get you the profits quicker than the average investor. I mean average investors get average results don't they?

What Is The One 'Thing', This "Trump Card Secret" of Successful Apartment Investors?

<u>A Motivated Seller!!</u>

Dear Friend:

A Heartland Of America Apartment Property Like The Shadowood Apartments Can Build Your Wealth, Predictably, Without Any Management Needed On Your **Part.**

You know how is goes. Many times you may be able to find those properties that seem to look "OK", but, you then find out the seller IS NOT motivated to sell the property.
The owner has it on the market and if it does sell for the price they are looking for, GREAT, if not, no big deal.

You Want to Make Sure You Do Everything You Can To Work With A Motivated Owner! And I Have A Motivated Owner Ready To Work With You...

If you don't work with a motivated owner it is difficult to negotiate great prices and terms that can build your wealth as quickly as possible. Or, in other words you will be dealing with the slow way to wealth, the average way.

The Faster, Less Stressful, Management Free Way To Apartment Property Wealth— The Shadowood Apartments Fit This Bill To A "T" - ESPECIALLY If You Have Been Wanting To Get Into Apartments

So, lets get down to it. Lets talk about the 84 unit Shadowood Apartment property that you requested information on. The information will reveal how YOU are going to get a Guaranteed Profit! Why? A motivated seller AND a great property! You see, the current owner of this property is only the second owner of the property. Heck, he has had it almost 25 years. Now, as you can imagine, his personal life and retirement are starting to become very important to him. He also wants to travel, vacation, see friends, grandkids, help with charitable causes, etc.

So, what's holding him back? What is keeping him from enjoying his retirement to the fullest? —

Its The Apartments!

Admittedly, he is not tied down to the property, but, at his age its always there. Needing attention, supervision, etc. So much so that he thinks it is keeping him from all "later in life activities" he really wants to do. So, because he feels that he is missing out—he is motivated to move the property. He has not problem in helping the buyer MAKE MONEY WHEN YOU BUY!

Exhibit #1 (continued)

So, What Is The REAL Story With This Property AND Why IS It Such A Good Deal?

Well, first, let me tell you what this property is NOT!:

- Not An Old Property — This ALL BRICK Apartment Was Built in 1975 So You Will Get Great Appreciation
- Not Some Weird Converted House Or Commercial Building — No Large Maintenance Bills

- Not A Hassle To Manage— Good Location And Tenant Mix. Management Is In Place So You Do Not Have To Worry About ANY Management.
- Not A Money Drainer — Tenants pay all utilities except water and garbage. No heating or cooling bills for the owner!
- Not Much Competition! — There is a new apartment property across the street BUT it rents for hundreds of dollars more per month than the Shadowood. This is good news! In an economic downturn would you rather rent a $700 apartment or a $500 apartment? I know which one I would want.
- Not In A Bad Location!— The location is excellent! Close to major shopping, employment, etc. The location, more than anything, is probably the best "non-financial" part of this property.
- Not Expensive — The property is priced at only $36,000 per unit! When is the last time you saw a price per unit that low??
- Not Risky — If you are conservative like me you want to avoid real estate risk as much as possible. The Shadowood is the ultimate "low risk" apartment property for reasons I will be describing in this report. Lets just say this is one of the best places to 'park your money' that I have had come along in a long time.

> No one comes close to understanding apartments, cash flow and present and future profits like Darin Garman. The success I have had with him in the past has made me a believer in his apartment property purchasing programs, especially if you do not want any management headaches...
>
> *Jason Rogers*

The fact that the owner has completely updated the property (roof, carpets, grounds, etc.) over the last year or so makes this even more interesting. Keeping capital improvement expenses at a minimum is always a great bonus. So, we not only have an all brick property, but, we have new roofs too!

So, we have an apartment property that cash flows from the get go AND is in practically "Turn Key' condition too? The Heartland has its advantages, and this is definitely one of them.

Take a look at these numbers and tell me where have you found this kind of cash flow and return recently?

Shadowood Cash Flow— $511,224 Annual Gross Income From The Apartment Complex

$271,480 Annual Expenses (Including Vacancies)
$239,743 Net Income

−$200,813 Debt Service of 75% Loan at 6.25%, 20 YR. Amortization
$38,930 Conservative 5% Cash Flow Or Cash On Cash Return
+
$59,403 Loan Principal Tenants Pay Down In Year 1 (It gets bigger every year)

(continued on next page)

Exhibit #1 (continued)

+

$61,040 Appreciation 1st Year at a conservative 2%   =

Total Cash Flow $159,300   OR A 20+% Total Return on a $763,000 investment!
(In pocket And on Paper)

AND THESE NUMBERS ARE CONSERVATIVE!! NO BLUE SKY HERE AT ALL!

To be honest with you I will be shocked if this apartment property is still on the market within a week after this letter goes out. With a flexible owner, this kind of conservative Heartland cash flow and return plus a price of $3,052,000 (that's only $36,000 per unit!!), it will not last long.

As an aside, when is the last time you found a property like this for only $36,000 per unit??

So, If This Deal Is So good, Why Is It Still On The Market AND Why Haven't YOU Bought It Garman??

Well, this is a fair question. Let me give you three reasons:

1) It is just becoming available. It has been on the market less than 90 days and I have just closed on two other deals. Frankly, I don't have all of the $750,000 required to buy the property right now. I just put some large chunks into some other deals.

2) I had one investor that took a look at it and wanted to buy BUT changed his mind to buy MORE apartments. It turned out to be too small for him. He wanted over 120 units.

3) Really, a large reason is that I wanted to get this deal in front of you. You have had an interest in apartment properties in the past and have responded. I knew that a lot of people would think this is a good deal and wanted "MY LIST" to get a shot at this one too!

4) I am willing to purchase AND oversee management of this property. I do want in on this deal too. But, I admittedly cannot do it alone. I have too many other irons in the fire right now with other properties to take this one on all by myself.

> *(You should feel pretty good about this. I would NOT put my own money and my own time overseeing the management of this property unless I really thought it was a good deal. You see, I am willing to put my own money, my own time into this deal too)*

Think about this—with a property with average rent of $500+ per month (it should be more) do you think you would have a harder time filling these apartments in any downturn or the units that rent for $600—$700 per month? This property is perfect for the current budget conscious tenant now AND in any potential tough economic time. Also, less turnover means less management hassles and expenses.

Q and A

Question 1.....

So, what makes this property a must for someone who wants to be a successful apartment investor, especially the investors that own those "AUTO PILOT" kinds of apartments you talk about?

Exhibit #1 (continued)

Here are a few reasons....
- 84 Units—Does NOT Require A Huge Management Staff and The Headaches Associated With IT <u>AND NO Hassles For You Since Management Is In Place—You Would Not Even Have To Deal With Management</u>

- Over 19% Total Return ON Investment—Quick Wealth Builder (SEE MY RETURN GUARANTEE LATER IN THIS LETTER)

- Great Passive Income Investment With Low Risk

- Quick Return Of Investment—Reducing Risk No Matter Your Age Or Economic Circumstance

- Great Location—Close To Tenant Conveniences—Which Makes It Easier On Turnover

Question 2....

What makes this the kind of property that even say 'millionaire apartment investors' would put their money into? C'mon, if that was REALLY the case, it would be gone by now.

Do you think the owner would have built and held onto the property for this long if it was not the case? He is grudgingly selling the property. Has been a part of his life for over 25 years and if he was younger would still keep it. The combination of full occupancy, all of the recent improvements, location, condition and management in place make it really worth a look - also....

- Its Easy To Be An Active Owner In This Property—A Great Wealth Builder Kind Of Property.

- No Surprises...Cash Flow And Return Are Pretty Much Predictable.

- Over 90% Occupied With A Great Reputation In The Community For Occupancy

- More Tenants To Fill Vacancies Here.. In Other Words, More Prospective Tenants Will Want To Pay Less Than $600 Per Month; So, You Will Have More People Looking At Vacancies vs. The Competition. So, You Know Your Phone Will Always Be Ringing Off The Hook With Prospective Tenants.

- No Terrorist Activity. Look, I Know You May Think This Sounds Silly, But, I Am Getting The Question More And More. I Doubt That Iowa Is On The Terrorist Radar Screen.

- Family And Schools. Arguably Iowa Is The Best Place To Raise A Family, Have Great Schools And Have A Pretty Much Stable Lifestyle. This Also Transcends Into The Types Of Tenants You Could Expect To Get And The Overall Economic Climate

- Less Risk With Your Money. I will go into this in more detail later.

Question 3....

The way you talk about this property Mr. Garman it sounds like the mythical "magic pill." Cut through all of the puffery and let me know what its REALLY LIKE..

Look, I know you may be thinking that I am talking "blue sky" here, but stay with me a

Exhibit #1 (continued)

minute.

Listen, I'm a serious apartment investor as well. I've worked with investors that have purchased millions of dollars of great apartment properties. I've looked at these properties cautiously, skeptically, and spent a ton of time analyzing them and feel that this apartment property has the best capability for wealth building and passive income and return for the smart investor...especially for the admittedly LAZY apartment investor— than any other on the market today.

I would even go so far to say that if you don't at least seriously consider this opportunity then you probably are not that serious about building your wealth. I'm serious...the "wealth building factor" as well as the absence of ongoing repair, management and maintenance issues (save time for your lifestyle) make this one that needs to be looked at further...

Question 4....

Do I Need To Put In $763,000? If Not, How Much Is The Minimum Investment I Can Put Down To Be A Part Of This? I Would Like To Spread My Risk.

I like to be conservative and 25% down payments are conservative. This means we would borrow 75% of the purchase price from a lender at the most competitive rate possible. (Remember, the price is $3,052,000) But, do you need the whole $750,000? The answer is no. If you want the property all to yourself, then, yes, you would be looking at putting $750,000 into this property.

But if that is not you....How much do you have to come up with?

I want a maximum of 15 people in the deal. That is a MAXIMUM! So, that means a minimum of $50,000 investment into this apartment business venture, our group that will be purchasing the property. Of course, you can go higher than $50,000. Your ownership in the property will of course be based on how much down payment (investment) you have in the deal. But it has to be a minimum of $50,000.

Question 5...

Why Should I Look At This vs. Stocks, Bonds Or Mutual Funds. Or Even Property In My Market For That Matter?

If this is your thinking in many ways I can see why. It has been drilled into our heads from all different kinds of "experts" that this is the easy way to make good money over the next 10, 15 or 20 years. That you need to wait this long and play it safer AND in these cases - you do not even have to deal with any management. Well, if you want to do what the average person does you will get average results. If you are satisfied with average, quite frankly you should stop reading and put this report in the trash! Remember the nice thing about the Shadowood Apartments is:

1. Management is non-existent. You don't have to sacrifice your lifestyle.
2. Tax advantages. Remember, you can write off interest in depreciation. Its nice to have a $10,000 cash flow – in your pocket and when you are done with your tax return you LEGALLY show a $4,000 loss – meaning less income tax to pay! If you are a high income earner this should be very attractive for you.
3. Cash Flow and Returns! This will change your life. After you go into this with me, 'seeing the light', you will wonder why you did not do this years ago!

If you're interested in taking the faster, less stressful path to wealth, this is for you.

Exhibit #1 (continued)

The Key Is Acting Quickly

What I have discovered about making money and building wealth with apartments is that it is—Being able to act quickly and recognize opportunity before the "other investor" —— this more often than not separates the winners from the losers in the apartment business.

Warning! Are you still skeptical?

Well, I am about everything. As I said before, anytime I hear about some opportunity that could enhance my financial situation, I tend to be well, skeptical. Like you, I've been duped, had, and taken advantage of. In other words, I've been ripped off. So, if you've read this information and think this is too good to be true, that you want to believe this can work for you, BUT think there's some catch to it somewhere, something to hide, something that will surprise and disappoint you - STOP! Let me assure you that's not the case here.

I'll Back Up What I Am Saying With A Promise AND A Guarantee...

Just so you know that I am serious here on these properties AND after analyzing many apartments, I am here to tell you that this property is legitimate. The property *will* cash flow like I am saying (remember, I am being conservative here on purpose, so , the cash flow will probably be even better than I am telling you) . If at any time the property fails to meet your expectations or is not performing like I am describing in this report you can:

Guarantee #1

Call me during the first two years of ownership and I will cut you an instant cash flow check of $3,000! You are reading this correctly. If you decide to work with me in this apartment property venture (84 units) and it doesn't live up to your expectations, just a little, even after two years, I will cut you a hassle check of $3,000— no questions asked. AND... You still maintain ownership in the property, nothing there changes!!

OR

Guarantee #2

If the property does not perform as I say it will I will buy you out! At any time over the first two years of ownership, if the property is not performing as well as I said it would OR it is not producing the returns and cash flows that I am saying I will buy you out! So, if you put $50,000, $100,000 or $250,000 or $75,000— whatever, in on the Shadowood Apartments and it does not perform like I am saying, I will buy you out. So, your initial investment is basically guaranteed! How often do you find that in a property? How often to you find that anywhere?

To show you that I'm not just blowing smoke and what I am saying is true, I will also partner with you on this property AND take an ownership interest in it AND will oversee management. That's right, I will own the property with you giving you peace of mind that someone who actually is telling you this is a good deal ALSO has a vested interest in the property overseeing the day to day operations too. Would I invest my money in a property that is NOT going to make the wealth building sense that I am talking about here?

Would I put these kinds of guarantees on the line if the property would not perform like I say it will? Of course not.

So, lets summarize the guarantees. 1) During the first 24 months, if the property is NOT cash flowing as I said it will, at your option, you can request an instant $3,000 cash flow check from me... OR

Exhibit #1 (continued)

2) After 24 months of owning the property with me, if it is not operating the way that I am saying it will I will buy out your original investment in the property.

So, I want to know, where else can you get this kind of property, with this kind of guarantee??

Nowhere!

You Only Have Until August 19th to respond! Limited To The First 15.

That is correct. Why? Well two reasons. First is that I had 47 other people request this information. Second—I only need a MAX of 15 ready to go people to move forward. I am sure that many will want "IN" on this, so, delaying would not be a good thing here.

Also, by that date the owner may decide to take the apartments off of the market and concentrate on buying a farm. Remember, I said he was **_grudgingly_** selling this building(s) only because of lifestyle changes that have occurred. Don't get me wrong, he is motivated to move the apartments now, but may be less motivated once some other details are taken care of and the drop dead date there is August 19th. So, act now.

OK Darin, I am interested, what do I do now?

1. Take a look at this letter again to make sure you understand everything involved in this apartment property.
2. Take a close look at the accompanying property information
3. Once you've satisfied yourself with all the materials AND THIS IS SOMETHING THAT YOU FEEL YOU SHOULD TAKE THE NEXT STEP ON...call immediately #319-378-6643 and tell Eileen you want the "Shadowood LLC Kit" OR FAX the enclosed registration form to #319-861-5659. 24 hrs.

Since we are limiting this to 15 people I need to have a "reservation deposit" of $500 per person, that is payable to Real Estate Marketing Systems via credit card or check. THIS DEPOSIT WILL NOT BE CHARGED OR CASHED UNTIL YOU REVIEW AND APPROVE EVERYTHING IN THE "SHADOWOOD LLC KIT". It is simply your reservation deposit on one of the 15 positions.

I am sure you will agree that we need to deal with serious people. This is the way to separate the serious vs. not so serious. IF you are one of the first 15 to respond AND you approve of everything in the Shadowood Kit, the $500 will be applied to your investment. If you reserve your space and you do not approve, your check will be returned and/or your credit card will not be charged. I can no longer take verbals without registration fees, sorry. So...

**If you are "IN" on this deal at this point, YOU need to RESERVE YOUR POSITION IN THE LLC RIGHT NOW! See the registration form for instructions...NOW!

The Shadowood kit will outline in detail how the investment would work, how to get involved in this property, LLC information, etc. AND what all of your costs, guarantees, obligations, etc. would be. Its basically the complete and detailed outline of how the purchase of the property would work in our Shadowood business venture and everything you need to know to make the Final "GO" decision on this.. You are not committed at this point, only, you are serious enough to reserve your 1 of 15 spots AND take an in depth look at how it would work for you.

Don't Do What Most People Will Do, Put It Off Until Tomorrow

I would not procrastinate on this. I expect a very good response AND many other investors wanting to check it out. So, don't delay—look over everything and fax me the enclosed response for to 319-861-5459 or call

Exhibit #1 (continued)

me direct at 319-378-6643.

Lastly, One Persons Problem Can Be Another Persons Opportunity

I know its not fair but this is reality. This is the world we live in. One persons desire for a simpler life (retirement) can be another's advantage (buying at a profit). This property is no different. So..

- Benefits Of Active Ownership Of A Great Property But Being A Passive Participant...

- Only $36,000 per unit...

- Good Cash Flow and Return—Short AND Long Term...

- Motivated Owner...Wants It To Move...

- Management In Place...Your lifestyle Does Not Change...

- Real Bankable Guarantees...Unlike All Those Other "Investments"

- Great Tax Advantages...Less Taxable Income to Report To Uncle Same

- You Are Considered An Active Owner...Even When You Are Seeking Passive Income

- Own The Property In An LLC...Shelters You From Liability.

- Have An Expert Running The Show Who Can Be At The Property In Ten Minutes...Making Sure I Am Always Watching Out For Profits.

..........Seize the day. I know that these kinds of apartment deals do not come along very often. You can bet others that are receiving this will be racing to get the Shadowood LLC Kit....RACING!

Sincerely,

Darin Garman, CCIM

PS. It is perfectly OK to make good money and have nice apartments that ALSO have good cash flow. Kind of like having your cake AND eating it too. There is no penalty to own this kind of cash flow apartment property, especially with the property having the capability of giving you more time to spend on other things!

PS #2 Most "investment" talk has always been about traditional investments like stocks, bonds, mutual funds, and maybe even single-family homes or some other kind of investment real estate, which was probably somewhere in your local market. Maybe you've heard of some single-family home investors and some of the profits that they have been able to make right there in your own market. But, when it came to the cash flow, instant equity profits, and quick returns...these "heartland" investment profits will make you wonder why you have not done this before.

PS #3. Remember, most **average** people will put this letter on their desk and get back to it later.

Exhibit #1 (concluded)

1

VIP Action Shadowood LLC Kit Registration Form

Say "YES" Now and Reserve Your Spot By Receiving Shadowood
Apartments LLC Kit That Details <u>ALL</u> Parts Of The Transaction
AND How You Can Get In On IT!

Please check all that apply: (Remember, there is no obligation at this point but please
be sincerely interested in this to get the LLC Kit)

☐ **I am basically IN on the Shadowood Apartments**. Enclosed is my credit card info for
$500 to hold my spot as one of the first participants in this apartment buisness venture.
By sending this I am guaranteeing a position to be IN the group. I understand that, if
after I receive the Shadowood LLC Kit I do not have an interest I can then decline and
there will be no charge against my card.

☐ I am not interested in this deal for my own reasons but please keep me posted on
others like it.

☐ **I am basically IN on the Shadowood Apartments**. Enclosed is a check for $500 to
hold my spot as one of the first participants in this apartment buisness venture. By
sending you this $500 check I am guaranteeing a position to be IN the group. I
understand that, if after I receive the Shadowood LLC Kit I do not have an interest I can
then decline and receive my check back uncashed.

Name _____

Mailing Address _____

Phone (in case I have questions) _____

Credit Card # _____ Expires_____

Fax this form to #319-861-5659

Or send to:
    Darin Garman, CCIM
    116 3rd St. SE
    Cedar Rapids Iowa 52401

SECTION TWO

The Kennedy System

Get "Into" the Customer

An old adage says that you can't understand someone until you've walked a mile in their shoes.

It's a good adage. We entrepreneurs, for instance, would be much better off if each of our elected representatives had to spend a couple of weeks every year running a small business, struggling to meet a payroll, and filling out a slew of government forms. The people trying to work their way out of the slums would be much better off if each of our elected officials had to go live with them for a week or two every year. And our farmers would get some of their problems solved if each of those same officials had to spend a week every year working on a farm. A number of well-run companies require their top executives to take customer complaint calls periodically, open and read mail from customers, even get out into the stores and deal with customers face-to-face.

The goal is *understanding*. To persuade someone, to motivate someone, to sell someone, you really need to understand that person.

How easy is it to miss? I wrote a TV infomercial script (essentially, a sales letter that comes to life) selling a product related to home mortgages. The script called for the spokesperson to walk into a living room, saying, "Here, in a typical American home . . . " The producer filmed this line with the spokesperson stepping into a white-carpeted room with a grand piano as its centerpiece! Out of touch, out of touch! Admittedly, most marketers are never that far out of touch with their customers or prospects, but make a mental note: the more in touch you are, the more probable your success. In my Copywriting Mastery Seminar (which hundreds of people pay $2,000.00 each to attend), I provide a special checklist of smart questions to ask about your customers and prospects. That checklist is reprinted here, as a very valuable "bonus" with this book.

By the way, my Copywriting Seminar in a Box and other resources for copywriters can be found at *www.dankennedy.com*. You should also register for the free 12-Week Sales Letter Writing e-mail course at *www.Ultimate-Sales-Letter.com*.

My "10 Smart Market Diagnosis and Profiling Questions"

1. What keeps them awake at night, indigestion boiling up their esophagus, eyes open, staring at the ceiling?
2. What are they afraid of?
3. What are they angry about? Who are they angry at?
4. What are their top three daily frustrations?
5. What trends are occurring and will occur in their businesses or lives?
6. What do they secretly, ardently desire most?
7. Is there a built-in bias to the way they make decisions? (Example: engineers = exceptionally analytical)
8. Do they have their own language?
9. Who else is selling something similar to them, and how?
10. Who else has tried selling them something similar, and how has that effort failed?

So, Step 1 in our system is to analyze thoroughly, understand, and connect with the customer.

In some cases, you may have a lot of demographic and statistical data about your customers or prospects available from your own records or from the vendors of the mailing lists you are using. You might (and probably should) know the ages, incomes, hobbies, and political affiliations of the people you're writing to—even what magazines they read regularly. Ideally, you can even get beyond this data and gain a "feeling" for these people. If you have none of this, if you have nothing but Zip Codes, I'd suggest getting into your car and driving slowly through the neighborhood of one of those Zip Codes, several times, on different days, to try to get a feel for those people. Or, if you're marketing to businesspeople, attend their meetings, read their trade journals.

I've spent 20 years working with the visualization techniques developed by Dr. Maxwell Maltz, author of the 30-million-copy bestseller, *Psycho-Cybernetics*, and I use those techniques—like "Theater In Your Mind"—to visualize my letter's recipients as living, breathing, thinking, feeling, walking, talking human beings. I visualize their day's experience. How did it start out? What did they do when they first arrived at the office? Do they get their mail presorted? Opened? From an "in" basket? Hand-delivered? When do they get it? Where will they stand or sit when going through it? At that time, what else are they thinking about? Preoccupied with? What do they worry about, complain about, secretly wish for, enjoy? Through this stretch of my own imagination, I try to become one with my letter's recipients, so I can anticipate their thoughts and reactions. If you don't have enough information and experience to do this, you must get it! I try to accept assignments to write sales letters only to types of prospects I know well. But given an assignment aimed at people I didn't understand, I'd go get that understanding.

Over the years, I've written hundreds of sales letters to Realtors. My clients have included the best-known sales trainers, seminar speakers, and marketing advisors to the real estate profession, including Craig

Forte, publisher of the "Service For Life" newsletter; Craig Proctor; and Tracy Tolleson's Pinnacle Club. I am not and have never been in the real estate business. When I first had to write a series of letters to Realtors, I knew nothing about their business. What did I do? I went to the public library and read several years' back issues of the trade journals that real estate agents subscribe to and read. One of the largest real estate companies had its convention in my city, so I went and hung out in the hotel lobby and bars and eavesdropped on conversations. I took a real estate agent to lunch and pumped him for information. I got myself to the point at which I could visualize myself as a real estate agent, speak the language of a real estate agent.

Once you've begun that process of identification, you'll be in a good position to determine what your letter's recipient wants. Write down these items in order of priority.

What Is Most Important to Your Reader?

There is a classic sales legend about the hot-shot salesman pitching a new home heating system to a little old lady. He told her everything there was to tell about BTUs, construction, warranties, service, and so on. When he finally shut up, she said, "I have just one question—will this thing keep a little old lady warm?"

Each time I've gone shopping for a personal computer, I've seen the same selling error repeated over and over again in the computer stores I've visited. These salespeople tell me everything about what's important to them, but they never slow down long enough to find out what's important to me.

The mistake is even easier to make in crafting a sales letter, because there's no possibility of corrective feedback from the customer during the presentation. That's why you must determine accurately, in advance, what their priorities are. And you must address their priorities, not yours.

I was once asked to write a corporate fundraising letter for the Arthritis Foundation's annual telethon in Phoenix. In examining samples of letters that other nonprofit organizations sent to corporate donors, I noticed that they all had this failing in common: they talked at great length about their own priorities—what they needed the money for, how it would be used, how funds were low, and so on—but they hardly addressed the donor's priorities at all. So I visualized myself as the business owner or executive being banged at by all these worthy charities' pleas and asked myself: "If I were to give, what would be important to me?" I came up with this list:

1. What benefit to me or my company justifies the cost?
2. Who else had picked this drive to contribute to? (How can I validate my judgment?)
3. How would I get the money to give? (What budget would it come out of? What other expense would have to be reduced to afford this new one?)

With that list in mind, I wrote the letter reproduced on the following pages, Exhibit #2. It garnered a response of only .5 percent, but the responses were from important new donors—one of whom contributed $13,000.00. This one new donor's contribution covered about half of all the costs of the local telethon that year. Perhaps most important, every expert associated with this project believed that such a letter would not work at all. Their previous experiences told them so. And in terms of return on investment, it was the most successful fundraising effort ever mounted by this local chapter. So why did this letter work where others had failed? Because it directly addressed the interests of the recipient, not the sender!

Get a fix on the prospect/customer/client, and on his or her desires; failing to do so will undermine all your other efforts.

Exhibit #2

_____ Director of Marketing

Dear _____:

Special, **highly effective TV exposure** at half the ordinary cost, even a smaller fraction of the ordinary cost—even free! Yes, it is possible.

Our annual **ARTHRITIS FOUNDATION TELETHON** has moved to CHANNEL 10 (Phoenix' CBS affiliate), and we are offering an expanded, more flexible, more creative range of Sponsor Opportunities to businesses of all sizes in the valley.

Many corporate sponsors last year actually participated spending little or no money—the funds were raised through fundraising events or promotions involving their employees or customers. For example, one major corporation used several Employee Promotions, and raised over $50,000.00. A small company used a Bowl-A-Thon with their employees, employees' family members, and friends, and raised $5,000.00. Both received excellent exposure on the Telethon. **AND THIS YEAR, THE OPPORTUNITIES ARE EVEN GREATER.**

There are many different Sponsor Programs available including several that give you a competition-free exclusive position. Sponsors are needed for each hour for the phone banks; for the Interview Area, where guests are interviewed by celebrity hosts; for table banners; and much more. There are even a few 1 and 2 minute Video Presentation Opportunities (company exposure) available. In all cases, representatives of your firm come on the show for you, your people, and your products. We will also assist you every step of the way with your employee fundraising event or other promotion, to raise the funds for your sponsorship. There really is no good reason not to participate.

As a sponsor, you'll be showing your concern for the community, in connection with a situation that, at one time or another, will affect over 35% of all families! Arthritis is one of the most common, frustrating, debilitating diseases. It is understandably of great concern to a great many people. Also, the Arthritis Foundation has an excellent track record in terms of appropriate use of funds for research and education

Exhibit #2 (concluded)

(rather than organizational overhead). We believe that real cures for arthritis are just around the corner; you can help get us there!

With our Telethon on Channel 10, we will benefit from their superior production capability, involvement of their popular celebrities, and advance promotional opportunities. Our Telethon will be on for several hours immediately before and again immediately after an NBA Basketball Game, which we believe will increase our viewership. And, of course, we're mixing our live, local show with a "feed" from the National Telethon, featuring major Hollywood entertainers. Everything points to our highest, most responsive viewership ever!

You'll be in good company, too, with local and national sponsors like: **Thrifty, Sears, Allstate, Greyhound, Prudential, and Procter & Gamble.**

To summarize, you have an opportunity to . . .

1. Help a good, worthy cause
2. Gain valuable TV exposure and publicity
3. Get all the benefits with little or no money out of your present budget—we'll work with your employees to raise the funds!
4. Possibly have exclusive position, if you act quickly
5. Have complete, step-by-step assistance from our staff

Why not give me a call; let's arrange a meeting where I can personally explain the different "standard opportunities" available and then "brainstorm" with you about the best way for your business to participate. There's no obligation, of course, and certainly no pressure, but, together, we just may figure out the perfect situation for your business.

Thank you for you consideration,

Joel L. Beck
Telethon Chairman for the Arthritis Foundation

JLB/va

Letter reprinted with permission of Dan Kennedy (writer) and Joel Beck, former telethon chairman, Arizona.

How an Outsider Becomes an Insider

Here's a letter I got from Jerry Jones, president of a direct-marketing and coaching company providing services to dentists nationwide:

"Back in 1997, after about 2 months of owning this business, I read the '10 Smart Questions' [in this chapter]. The list exposed my biggest handicap in marketing to dentists: not being one of them. Because I'm not the customer in my niche, I have had to work hard at understanding what motivates them, keeps them awake at night, what the current desirable carrot is to them. Here are six things I do to stay in that frame of mind. And I'm apparently managing to do it, because I am frequently accused of being a dentist!

1. I read EVERY industry publication EVERY month.
2. I visit Web sites that host discussion forums for dentists.
3. I subscribe to e-mail groups where only dentists communicate back and forth.
4. I attend industry functions, conventions, seminars, and trade shows.
5. I "play prospect" with other product and service providers to dentists.
6. I routinely "mastermind" with dentists, and with other marketers and vendors who provide services to the profession.

I think this is so important that, most recently, I've even invested in three dental practices, to get more firsthand understanding, and to have laboratories to test my new strategies, ideas, direct-mail campaigns, and products."

Jerry's an extremely astute marketer who has enjoyed enormous success doing something that is generally difficult to do: becoming a respected, sought-after coach, consultant, and guru to a profession he's never been a part of. It's far more common for the guru to have come up through the same industry, to have been where his students and clients are. My Platinum Member Ron LeGrand, author of the book *How to Be a Quick Turn Real Estate Millionaire*, is a good example. Today, he teaches tens of thousands of people how to start and prosper in real estate investing and "flipping," and people routinely spend $5,000.00 to $15,000.00 attending his "boot camps." Ron was an auto mechanic when he saw a newspaper ad for a real estate seminar, went to the seminar, and struggled to buy his first property. He has since done more than 1,600 deals himself. He is very much in tune with his customers because he was one of "them," and is still very active in the same businesses they're in.

What Ron and Jerry have in common—although they get to it by different paths—is a deep understanding of their customers.

Get "Into" the Offer

Just as you try to crawl inside the letter recipient's mind and heart, you want to crawl around in your product or service, too.

If you're writing a letter to promote a product, you need to get the product, use it as the consumer would, play with it, test it, take it apart and put it back together, even demonstrate it to others as a salesperson would. If you're writing a letter to promote a service, use the service yourself if possible. Go talk to those who use it. Talk to people who use a competitive service. If you're writing a letter to promote a special offer, do everything possible to analyze that offer. Try it out on people. Find out whether they understand it, whether they're intrigued by it.

Build a List of Product/Offer Features and Benefits

I like to put each item on a separate 3" × 5" card, so I can shuffle them after I've written them all out and sort them according to importance. This works better for me than does a list on a sheet of paper. Sometimes I tack the cards up in a vertical row on a bulletin board in my office so it's easy for me to keep looking at them as I write. This is essentially a brainstorming exercise. You can do it alone, aided by product literature, or you can do it with a group of participants. Either way, the idea is to list all possible features and benefits, then organize them by importance.

Note that I said "features and benefits." It's amazing how easily people fall into talking about the features of their product or service, instead of the benefits it provides. I find myself constantly reminding our clients: "People do not buy things for what they are; they buy things for what they do."

Resource!

For 50 examples of "Features Translated to Benefits" from actual, successful sales letters, go to *www.Ultimate-Sales-Letter.com* and enroll in the free 12-Week Sales Letter Writing e-mail course.

Now, here is an advanced copywriting secret, courtesy of my friend Ted Nicholas: the use of "the *hidden* benefit." Ted has personally sold more than $200 million worth of how-to books via direct-response ads in magazines and newspapers and via sales letters, and retired relatively young to Switzerland on the proceeds, so he knows a thing or two about salesmanship-in-print. Ted often looks for what he calls the hidden benefit to emphasize. This means it's not the obvious, first benefit that you think of, yet it is one that is of profound importance to your customer.

I'll give you an actual example. Pamela Yellen, the CEO of the Prospecting & Marketing Institute, based in Santa Fe, New Mexico, and I were conducting a multi-day seminar for her clients—corporate executives and general agents from life insurance companies—about new methods of recruiting agents. The attendees had paid a very high per-person fee to be there, most had traveled great distances, and the subject was of critical importance to them, yet we both noticed that on breaks, what most of them were talking about was where they were going to go play golf that evening when the seminar let out, the next morning before it started, or the day afterward. Both Pamela and I made note of how important it was to these clients of hers to get out on the golf course.

This led to one of the most profitable ads Pamela has ever written and run in her own industry's trade journals, with the headline: "Puts Recruiting On Auto-Pilot So You Can Go Play Golf!" The entire ad is reproduced in Exhibit #3. As you'll see, it sells the system we devised for insurance agent recruiting, but it does so circuitously, by emphasizing the hidden benefit: You'll get the job done with less time invested, so you can spend more time on the golf course.

Exhibit #3

Are you **tired** of **struggling** with recruiting? **Unexcited** about endlessly pumping everyone you know for names? **Burned-out** from **chasing after candidates** day after day? **FREE report** reveals how revolutionary Magnetic Recruiting System:

"Puts Recruiting On Auto-Pilot So You Can Go Play Golf!"

Exciting, new, but already proven system causes qualified, enthusiastic candidates to literally chase you down!

"I ran a small classified ad once in a Sunday paper and a series of inexpensive radio spots over the course of a week, according to the formula I learned from **Magnetic Recruiting**, and got 11 appointments from it. Every one of those people called me. 10 were excellent quality, not one single person was a no-show and I found three people worth hiring in the bunch! **Magnetic Recruiting** definitely causes a lot of excitement in the agency, gets the whole office involved, creates a lot of activity and attracts good, solid quality candidates." —George K., PA

"The candidates I see through Magnetic Recruiting are the types of candidates I really want to work with and the ones that stick. The system is consistent, predictable and attracts high quality candidates. It allows me to determine which river I'm going to pan gold from, as opposed to the hit-and-miss method we've been using in this industry, and how many gold nuggets are going to come out the other end. Magnetic Recruiting is a better way to pan for gold. Once it's set up in your agency, it's automatic."—Victor L. BC, Canada

"**Magnetic Recruiting** gets me an additional 18 to 22 booked appointments every month with some of the most exceptional candidates I've ever seen—and every one of them called ME! I'm seeing highly successful corporate executives and managers, bankers, attorneys and CPAs, successful sales professionals in other fields and business owners all the time now. Magnetic Recruiting saves me an inordinate amount of time, puts the entire process on auto-pilot and allows me to spend time on the right things. The candidates who come in to talk to me already know they're going to be selling insurance and financial services, and yet they usually try to convince me that they're the right person for the job!"—Tim M., OH

"**Magnetic Recruiting** maximizes recruiting efficiency by minimizing interviews with poor candidates. Eliminates the excuse of not having recruits to talk to."—Bob K., NC

"**Magnetic Recruiting** attracts some of the highest caliber candidates from cold sources I've ever seen. I routinely have executives in downsizing companies and others earning $100–$200,000 a year coming in to see me. For the first time I have people from cold sources seeking me out trying to convince me they're the one instead of me trying to sell them on the virtues of our career. It saves me a half day of work every week and my secretary handles it all. All I do now is accept candidates' calls and show up for the interview."—Saul C., NY

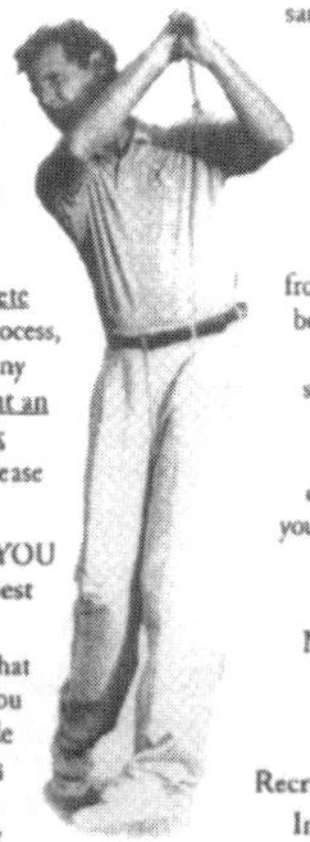

Would you like to have a predictable flow of interested, high-caliber candidates calling YOU and working hard to convince you to accept them? Dream candidates who already know what your opportunity is all about?

If you'd like to have complete control over your recruiting process, regardless of the economy or any other market condition and put an end to the endless grunt work you've become resigned to, please keep reading.

Getting Candidates to Call YOU Is Easy...If You Know the Best Kept Marketing Secret!

Maybe you too have found that recruiting is getting tougher. You have to talk to a lot more people than ever before. Maybe it's been awhile since recruiting was actually fun. Or, you may be in that happy minority having a great recruiting year. But you're still not where you want to be. Perhaps you're sick of pumping your agents and nominators for names. Chasing after people who aren't interested in hearing your story. Seminars that hardly seem worth the bother.

You see, success at getting plenty of qualified candidates has a lot more to do with understanding the real secrets of direct-response marketing...and little to do with chasing after prospects. Whether this is your first year in management, or you're a thirty year veteran, you will love to never again talk to anyone unless they have CALLED YOU!

Your Competition is Using These Magnetic Recruiting Techniques to Steal Your Best Prospects...With a Story Half as Good as Yours!

The business opportunity, franchise and distributorship industries are currently booming like never before. There are today far more people looking for you, than there are you looking for them!

So why is recruiting down? The biggest obstacle you face is marketing incest. Everyone goes to the same meetings, listens to the same speakers, reads the same publications. Just like when people inbreed, it doesn't take very long before everyone gets stupid. Breakthroughs come from going "outside the box" and bringing new, proven, translated systems back in. Keep doing what you've always done and you can be sure as shootin' you'll never get anything different than what you've already got.

Now There's a New, 100% Measurable Replacement For Old-Fashioned Recruiting Grunt Work!

Imagine how your life would be different if you only talked to candidates who CALLED YOU, and were really interested in your opportunity! Do you think you'd feel more successful if you didn't need to constantly badger everyone for names? This is no pipe dream.

FREE Report Tells All!

You can be the greatest manager in the world—but that won't do you a bit of good if you can't attract enough of the right people. So, if you are ready to discover the astonishing secrets of getting qualified candidates to call you, CALL NOW!

1-800-856- (US and Canada), 24-hours-a-day for FREE recorded message and to get your FREE Report!

Or, write "Recruiting" on your business card and fax to

Create a Damaging Admission and Address Flaws Openly

This may seem strange to you at first, but identifying the flaws in your product, service, or offer is a big step forward toward making the sale!

By acknowledging the flaws, you force yourself to address your letter recipient's questions, objections, and concerns. You also enhance your credibility.

Figure Out Why They Won't Respond

People are damned contrary creatures! You present them with a perfectly good offer and they still don't respond. Why not? Yogi Berra said, "If people don't want to come out to the ballpark, nobody's gonna stop 'em." Well, there are lots of reasons to come to the ballpark. Again, I like to use 3" × 5" cards and put a reason for not responding on each card. I try to think of every possible objection, concern, fear, doubt, and excuse someone might use to keep from responding.

I talked with a doctor about a particular product being marketed through the mail by a company competitive with my own. The doctor told me that he had received at least a dozen sales letters from that company, had read them, and was interested in the product, and I knew he had the financial ability to buy. So why hadn't he? He told me that he felt the offer was too good to be true, and that made him skeptical about everything said about the product. If the marketer had anticipated that reaction and answered it somewhere in his letter, he would certainly have increased the response to his mailings.

Honestly Assess the Disadvantages of Your Offer and Face Them

Every product, service, and offer has some unattractive points. Nothing's perfect, and everybody knows that. By admitting and openly discussing the drawbacks to your offer, your "credibility stock" goes way up on most of your letter recipients' charts. This is sometimes called "damaging admission copy." Consider this example, from a sales letter sent to area residents by a small Italian restaurant:

> . . . if you want waiters in tuxedos with white linen cloths over their arms, menus with unpronounceable words all over them, and high-priced wines served in silver ice buckets when you go out for Italian food, our little restaurant is not the place to come. But if you mostly want good, solid, home-cooked pasta with tasty sauces made with real vegetables and spices by a real Italian Mama, and will trade white linen for red and white checked plastic tablecloths, you'll like our place just fine. If you're okay with a choice of just two wines, red or white, we'll give you as much of it as you want, from our famous bottomless wine bottle—free with your dinner . . .

This restaurant owner took competitive disadvantages and turned them into a good, solid, "fun" selling story.

Get Your Sales Letter Delivered

Early in the process of putting together your sales letter, you need to think about getting the finished letter into the hands of people who can respond.

There is a very real, significant mail nondelivery problem in this country. Various studies and audits conducted by the Postal Service, the Direct Marketing Association, and others indicate that 10 to 30 percent of properly addressed third-class mail never reaches its intended recipients! I believe the problem is even worse. Postal employees actually discard or deliberately destroy huge quantities of what they perceive to be "junk mail." Occasionally, news items verify this, with reports of postal workers caught with garages or barns full of undelivered mail. One erupted into fire from spontaneous combustion. I even know of incidents in which quantities of first-class mail were dumped. I have charted the same weird patterns of nonresponse to mass mailings sent first class as I have for bulk. I've also had this problem personally verified by a retired postal worker, now a client of mine in his post-retirement business. Mailing first class, preferably with an actual stamp rather than a meter imprint, tremendously improves your odds of delivery, but it's still no guarantee.

The postal service has been aggressively working on this problem and succeeding at reducing deliberate nondelivery. Improvements apparently have been made. I think the problems are less pervasive today than they were when I first wrote this book, but the risk of nondelivery remains. I even have some clients who now profitably use bulk mail. As recently as last year, however, I know personally of two very significant instances of deliberate nondelivery that sabotaged entire mailing campaigns. The worst part of this problem is that you might never know that your mailing was done in by nondelivery. So I still consider this when making all the decisions about the outside of the mailing piece.

Often I design envelope exteriors or mailer formats with fooling the postal worker in mind. The same design ideas that increase odds of delivery also seem to increase the odds of getting it opened and looked at, but, frankly, my big concern is successfully conning the postal workers!

I first discovered quite by accident that this could be done, and the story is instructive. These days, imitation overnight-express envelopes are quite common; you've undoubtedly seen them and probably received at least a few. But some years ago, I think before they existed or, at least, when they were still rare, I chose that format for a mailing. It was for a company called General Cassette Corporation, and we designed a red, white, and blue General Express Letter package. It featured pictures of jet airplanes and wording like: URGENT—OPEN IMMEDIATELY. The mailing was going to a thousand of the company's best clients and prospects, and it was going via cheap bulk mail.

The first thing that happened was that the supervisors at the Phoenix Bulk Mail Station refused to accept the things. I had to call our attorney, who got a directive from Washington, D.C., ordering the local station to accept the mail.

I quickly understood their reluctance. The morning after the bulk-mail drop, we started getting telephone calls from as far away as Boston and New York—from people who had received delivery of our Express Letter in the middle of the night, by the post office's express mail people! We were ultimately able to track more than 150 units that were handled and delivered as express mail—15 percent of the mailing. Much of the rest was apparently handled as first class, based on the quickness of the customer response. And virtually all of it got there. In fact, the mailing achieved an 82 percent response rate. I can just see a batch of eight or nine arriving at the Duluth post office: veteran carriers look at it and grumble, "Must be some new kind of express mail. As usual, nobody tells us anything. Better jump in the Jeeps and get these delivered pronto!"

The lesson I learned from that experience was that it is possible to con the postal workers into doing their job and delivering my mail. I've kept it in mind every time I've assembled a mailing since then. I suggest you do the same. Following are a few strategies that seem to work consistently.

The best counterattack options for the sales letter sender have to do with envelope design, but the design option you select directly affects the letter's theme and copy, so this selection must be an early step in the system. The point is that before you can get the deathless prose of your newborn sales letter read, you've got to figure out how to get the darned thing delivered.

First Class versus Bulk

Bulk's no bargain if you're hit with a 20 percent and up nondelivery factor, and my own experience indicates this may well be the norm. If you can possibly adjust the economics of your business to justify first-class postage, that's what you should use.

Live Stamps versus Meter Indices

The basic principle behind these strategies is that postal workers are least likely to dispose of mail they believe the recipients are expecting. Live stamps seem to suggest that only a small number of pieces were mailed and that they may be expected correspondence rather than "junk mail." Incidentally, automated stamp-affixing machines are readily available.

Individually or Ink-Jet Addressed Envelopes

A gummed white label is a dead giveaway in most cases. Recently, I had an interest in a business mailing as many as 25,000 hand-addressed envelopes a week. A whole neighborhood of stay-at-home moms picked up boxes of envelopes at the office each Monday, took them home, addressed them, were paid piece-meal, and brought them back on Wednesday. We knew from testing that it made enough of a difference in response to justify this extra effort.

The Sneak-Up Approach

A plain white envelope with no business name; only an address with no name or a person's name as the return address; no teaser copy; individual or ink-jet addressing; and a live stamp—all this makes your mailing look like a letter, not advertising or junk mail. It then stands the highest possible chance of completed delivery. Given that design and first-class postage, I'd give it a 98% chance of getting there and getting opened.

_____ Resource! _____

The leading vendor of personalized, pure "sneak-up" mailings is Think Ink. Its President, Craig Dickhout, is thoroughly versed in preparing, printing, and executing these kinds of mailings for clients from all over the world. You can get information and samples from Craig; fax a request to 714-374-7071.

Intimidating Imprints

"Audited Delivery . . . Verified Delivery . . . The Information You Requested Is Enclosed . . . Important Documents Enclosed . . ." Imprints or affixed gold seals with this kind of wording seem to work well. Exhibit #4 is one I received back in 1985, but the strategy hasn't changed, and these kinds of official-looking labels are frequently used in political, fundraising, and business-to-business mailings, to increase likelihood of delivery by the postal folks and by company mailroom clerks, secretaries, and other gatekeepers.

Exhibit #4

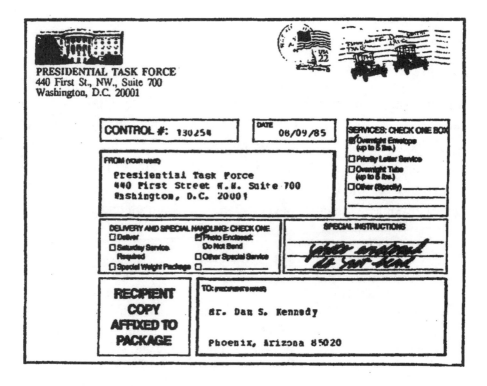

Get Your Sales Letter Looked At

Let's optimistically assume that the lion's share of your mail survives the determined destructiveness of our postal system and actually arrives at its intended destination. Now what?

Just about everybody throws out some mail unopened. Letters that do get opened and looked at have only a quick heartbeat to survive the sort, avoid the wastebasket, and earn the attention and interest of the recipient.

The best and most succinct advice I ever got on this subject is from a true direct-marketing genius, Gary Halbert. Gary says, "Picture the person you've sent your sales letter to with a stack of mail in his hands, sorting through that stack, standing next to a wastebasket." You might write up a sign and post it on your wall:

America sorts its mail standing over a wastebasket.

Wow! That is an insight worth a great deal of money. Think of it this way: People prejudge their mail, just as they do other people, places, books, and so on. That may be unfair or unreasonable, but it really happens.

If you're sending sales letters to businesspeople, consider that the mail may be screened by an assistant. If you survive that "cut," then your recipient sorts the envelopes—not the actual letters—standing over a wastebasket.

Even I, a mail junkie, student, and collector, have days and sometimes weeks when I am just too busy to open and look at every piece of mail that crosses my various desks. I receive mail at my Phoenix office, and personal mail at two different private mail services in my two home cities. During busy times, when I receive these boxes of mail, I stand right next to the waste can. The mail from my office has been presorted for me, divided into "Urgent," "Personal," "A-Pile Business," "Other," "Catalogs and Magazines." The other mail has not been presorted. So, if I'm really time-pressed, I create a new A pile, a B pile that will wait, and I ruthlessly discard as much as I can, unopened and unread.

Let me give you an example of how big an impact this can have. We have a business that mails extensively to doctors, and, over the years, I've tried every kind of envelope look that you can imagine. By far, the mailings that pull best are sent in "plain Jane" envelopes without our company name on them, but, instead, with a doctor's name and return address. These envelopes are not screened by staff. They get opened by the doctor. The response to these mailings versus the same letters sent in different, more "honest" envelopes is sometimes as much as 300 percent higher!

Mailing to consumers at their homes carries a different set of problems. First of all, it is my admittedly informal observation that in most households, most of the mail is sorted and handled by the woman, not the man. And today's extraordinarily busy working woman is ruthless in handling this mail. Much of it hits the trash without seeing the light of day.

So, how do you get your sales letter opened? The same strategies I just described for fooling postal employees also serve to motivate recipients to open the envelope. In addition, different sizes and colors of envelopes can add impact and gain attention. If you are going to use a devious strategy, the most important thing to remember is that you must quickly fulfill the envelope's promise inside. For example, when we mail with a doctor's name as our return address, we enclose a little scratchpad-sized "lift letter" from that doctor that says: "The information presented here has been of immense value to me and I thought it might interest you, also. The Publisher asked me to let you know how much I've gained from his service and I was glad to do so. You'll do yourself a favor by reading everything enclosed. Sincerely . . ." Similarly, if your envelope says "Personal" outside, there had better be something "personal" inside. Unfulfilled envelope promises destroy the credibility of everything enclosed and everything you have to say. Fulfilled envelope promises enhance your credibility.

The Opposite of Sneak-Up

In spite of everything said in this chapter and the preceding chapter, the overwhelming majority of direct mail *does* clearly identify itself as a salesperson arriving, complete with business identity, logo, and "teaser copy." My own tendency is to use the techniques discussed previously in these chapters when reaching out to new prospects for the first time, but to switch to using the outside of the envelope to get the reader excited and curious about what's inside when mailing to established customers who recognize and respect the sender. My rule is: Never be half pregnant. If you are going to reveal that you are sending business mail or sales material via a company name, meter imprint, or even one line of teaser copy, such as "Inside: 10 Ways To Cut Your Ad Budget By 70% But Sell More!" then you might as well use the entire envelope as a billboard and sell, sell, sell!

A good example is this envelope created for a client of mine, Rory Fatt, for a mailing about one of his seminars for restaurant owners. As you can see in Exhibit #5, the whole face of the envelope is a billboard. There's teaser copy, a photo of a car being given away—and note the personalization. Each recipient's name appears on the license plate of the car!

Because few restaurant owners have aggressive gatekeepers between them and their mail, and because Rory was mailing to clients he already has a relationship with, I advised this approach, and it was very successful. There is still risk of postal nondelivery, but there is high probability of the recipient being motivated to open it when it is received. If this was

Exhibit #5

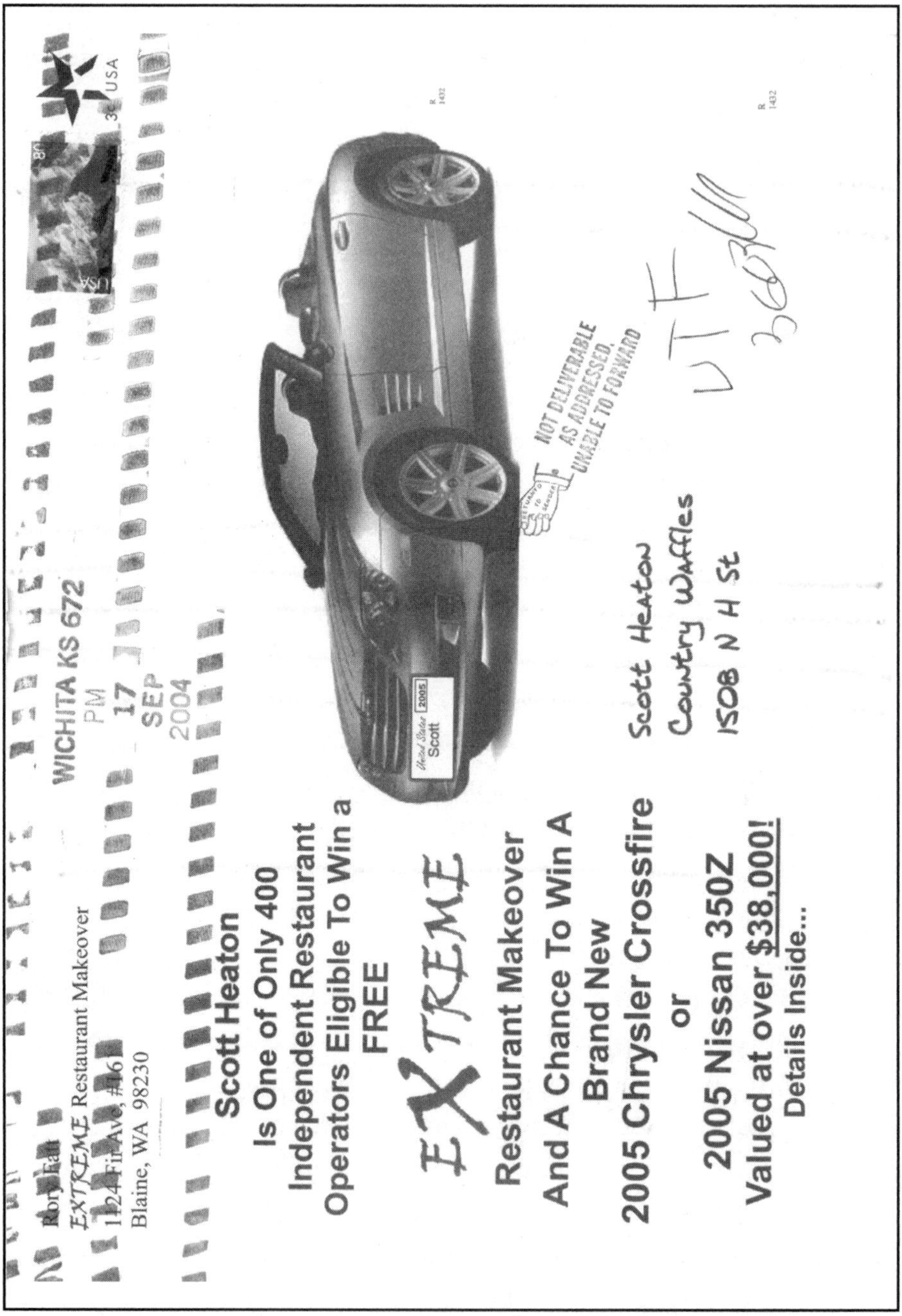
Rory Fatt
EXTREME Restaurant Makeover
1124 Fir Ave, #161
Blaine, WA 98230
WICHITA KS 672
PM
17 SEP
2004
Scott Heaton
Is One of Only 400
Independent Restaurant
Operators Eligible To Win a
FREE
EXTREME
Restaurant Makeover
And A Chance To Win A
Brand New
2005 Chrysler Crossfire
or
2005 Nissan 350Z
Valued at over $38,000!
Details Inside...
NOT DELIVERABLE
AS ADDRESSED,
UNABLE TO FORWARD
Scott Heaton
Country Waffles
1508 N H St

instead being sent to corporate executives who have a gatekeeper in the way, I might have put this envelope inside a simple brown kraft envelope, personally addressed, with Rory's name in the return address corner, and I might have sent it via Federal Express or Priority Mail, in those companies' outer envelopes.

As you can see, in each instance, I invest a great deal of thought into getting the mail delivered, and delivered to the targeted decision-maker—and you should too!

_____ **Resource!** _____

Would you like to know THE five simple words you can put on the outside of just about any envelope that will dramatically improve its "getting opened" numbers? Register to receive the free 12-Week Ultimate Sales Letter e-mail course at *www.Ultimate-Sales-Letter.com.* The answer's in the Module on "Envelopes."

The Power of Personalization

One of the latest discoveries that many of my clients are using is what I call a "hybrid envelope." It crossbreeds personalization with teaser copy. A leader in developing and using this approach is Bill Glazer. Shown here, in Exhibits #6 and #7, is the front and back of a 9" × 12" envelope sent to cold prospects (in this case, furniture store owners). The front is a window envelope with a personalized sales letter showing through. The city and state and the individual's name are in the letter's headline, and you can see "Dear Rebecca," in the window as well. Yes, each one is personalized, and the technology exists to do this easily. But also note that the front of the envelope has teaser copy too, which is printed in blue ink.

Then the back is printed as a billboard, every inch covered with testimonials.

I think you'll agree that this is an unusual and powerful approach.

Exhibit #6

BGS
8600 LaSalle Road
Chester Suite 321
Towson, MD 21286

Presorted
First Class
U.S. Postage
PAID
Permit #662
Wichita,

"How Bill Glazer Can Make The People Who Live
In Frankfort,KY Stand In Line And Beg
Rebecca Wall To Sell Them
All The Furniture In Their House"

Rebecca Wall
M Simon Furniture Co
226 Mero St
Frankfort KY 40601-1920
I.I..III....II..II......II...iIl.I...I.III....I.I.II..I.I..I

Dear Rebecca,

YOUR COMPETITION
DOES NOT
WANT YOU TO HAVE
THE INFORMATION
ENCLOSED!!

Exhibit #7

FIND OUT HOW THESE FURNITURE SHOP OWNERS HAVE DISCOVERED SUCCESS!!!

After spending many years interacting and working with the top copywriters and marketers in my business, your abilities are far superior to all the rest. Most so-called experts create information with no experience in the real world. You live and breathe every aspect of your business, and you have an amazing ability to translate your depth of knowledge into creating great events and promotions that garner high response rates from your customers.

– Sam and Leslie Fishbein / Kacey Fine Furniture

Bill,

just wanted to drop you and note to tell you that I took one of your mailings right out of your Marketing System, tweaked it for my furniture store, and it was the most successful promotion we have ever held.

We have also successfully used Voice Broadcast to our customers exactly how you teach it and added a 25% increase to an existing sale that we have held before.

Finally, I want to point out that we have implemented your "Customer Loyalty" program and not only do our customers love it, but it brings them back more frequently. As you can imagine, this is always a challenge in the furniture business.

Thanks for everything!

– Charlie Covington / Batesville Furniture

Every retailer needs a continuing source of new ideas, and Bill is one of the best sources I've found.

– John W. Cole / Walker Bros.

I'M A FURNITURE RETAILER. What I love about Bill Glazer's Marketing System is that he brings us fresh ideas from many different retail niches other then the 'same old, same old' that I see in furniture.

Since investing in the System, I've already implemented a Frequent Buyers Program designed to bring back existing customers more often, and a Referral Program designed to get my customers to refer their friends and family members to my store.

Perhaps the biggest change in thinking for me was Bill got me to understand that it was a lot less expensive to bring back previous customers instead of wasting time and money on "expensive" ads, trying to attract new customers.

– Ron Wessel / Love Furniture Galleries

Everyone can benefit from BGS Marketing materials. The chapters on referral programs and attracting customers by new associates are worth the price of admission. And, anyone considering cable TV must see the tape for great ideas.

– Andrew Mallor / Andrew Davis

The ideas, techniques, and strategies we've gleaned from Mr. Glazer have truly helped us re-design our approach to our total advertising efforts this year. Each time we follow Bill's lead, we end up with a greater focus and the results have shown in our written sales in our increase of 11.23% in the last 9 months (as compared to the same period the previous year).

– David Kessler / Flooring Xpress

After "72 years in business" we often have struggled to come up wit new promotions and events to bring our customers back on a more frequent and consistent basis. The BGS Marketing System has given us a real "shot in the arm." We have now developed a formal marketing committee that meets regularly to plan store events. While many of the concepts within the BGS had been practiced at our store, this introduced many new ways to approach them. We've completely reinvented our Rewards program, and we've activated a Referral System. Thanks BGS Marketing renewing the enthusiasm in our business.

– Daniel E. Reynolds / Stephenson's

The system has breathed new life into our business. The final reductions sale promotion alone has turned the "bad" months into my 3rd and 4th best months of the year. Now I have to plan off price buys just to keep up with demand! A good problem to have.

Independent business owners who do not have cookie cutter franchises are desperate for entrepreneurial direction and your counsel is the most comprehensive I have ever seen (I have 23 years experience). BGS Marketing keeps reminding us of the common sense marketing ideas we so often forget to use or, even worse, stop using because we are bored with those simple direct mail ideas or the secret possible scenarios – we are too lazy to use them. Even if you think your business is running at its peak, Bill's advertising ideas are guaranteed to improve your marketing efforts.

– Rob Herzog / Herzog's

Have been with BGS for close to a year. The parts that apply to my store are invaluable. They truly keep us focused. Our customer response to mailings has jumped from approximately 2% to as high as 10%

– G.A. Kouros / Katy's Boutique

Dear Bill,

We have been with your program a little over 2 years. It takes a while to become a believer even when we know that what we are told works. Last Christmas we did a 3-page letter following your strategies with and got a 16% plus return on the mailing. For a small community of less than 4,000 people we were ecstatic.

– Keith Bryan / Bryan's

I received your kit in middle of our 100th anniversary sale. It was, so far, a complete flop. The old newspaper ads no longer work. I studied your material day and night, hours & hours. Then I sent out a mailing using the exact techniques you teach. **Finally customers started coming in Prepared to Buy!** Thanks. It's great!

– Randall Richter / Richter Furniture

Your Marketing System is great! Everything is so well pre pared. The information is broken down from all facets of marketing is funneled down that enables me to take a new approach to my business. Thanks for all you do. (Any retailer not using your Marketing System doesn't know what they are missing.)

– Dick Lerner / Bel Air Fashion

We have utilized the BGS System for sometime now....The lowest common denominator is this - If you take one idea and change it slightly to match your personal style, you will find tremendous success. This system works.

– Tim Hare / Riverside Shop

– Jay Tollett / Collins & Williams

Bill-

Thanks to you and your marketing system we are not participating in the recession!

Operating as a family business for sixty-four years we were not accustomed to sales decreases, however after 9-11 our sales began to decrease-from 5% to 20% each month. We even had considered closing our business.

When we heard about the Bill Glazer Marketing System, we felt that this may be the solution to our problems. We knew that we were "up against a brick wall." And at least we needed to try the system.

After reading your manuals, and listening to you tapes, we began to implement some of the strategies. We began to see our sales increase - from a 20% decrease in November to a 3% increase in March, and a 16% increase in April 2003 over April 2002.

We are great thing ahead as we continue to implement more Bill Glazer Strategies! Sell and retire at seventy-six years old! Why we haven't touched the tip of the iceberg yet! Bill, thank you again.

– Lloyd Stephens / Stephens of Mendenhall, Inc.

YOU'LL FIND EVEN MORE SUCCESS STORIES INSIDE...

Get Your Sales Letter Read

In person-to-person selling, there is a little formula that is taught almost universally. It's called "AIDA," which stands for Attention, Interest, Desire, Action. This is the orderly process of a sale. So, once you've gotten the letter recipient's attention, you must work to develop his or her interest.

From Annoying Pest to Welcome Guest

One warm afternoon I was at home alone, sitting at my kitchen counter, a large iced tea in hand, talking on the telephone with an important client in another city. The doorbell rang. I ignored it. It rang relentlessly. I ignored it. Then the uninvited, unwanted pest pounded on the door. "Damn," I said to myself—but I still tried to continue my conversation. Suddenly there was someone banging on the sliding glass door behind me; at this stage it was a contest of wills and I refused to even turn around and look. Then he was back banging on the front door. I finally excused myself from the conversation and went to the door to get rid of this guy.

He was a passing motorist trying to tell me that the shrubs along my backyard wall were in flames!

Suddenly this guy was elevated in status from annoying pest to welcome guest! Clearly, he was on my side: "Get the hose going—I'll call the fire department!" Together we kept the burning shrubbery from setting my whole house on fire.

How did he go from pest to welcome guest so quickly? Because he had something to tell me that I instantly recognized as of urgent importance and of great value and benefit to me.

In case you had illusions to the contrary, no one is sitting around hoping and praying that they will receive your sales letter. When it arrives, it is most likely an unwelcome pest. How do you earn your welcome as a guest? By immediately saying something that is recognized by the recipient as important and valuable and beneficial.

I received a letter with this warning across the top:

WARNING: THIS LETTER IS IMPREGNATED WITH A HAZARDOUS CHEMICAL ACTIVATED IF DISCARDED UNREAD. MINUTES AFTER BEING DISCARDED, THE LETTER'S CHEMICAL WILL INTERACT WITH OTHER COMPONENTS IN YOUR WASTEBASKET AND EXPLODE INTO A GIANT GRIZZLY BEAR THAT MAY EAT YOU ALIVE. FOR YOUR OWN SAFETY AND THE SAFETY OF THOSE AROUND YOU, DO NOT DISCARD THIS LETTER UNREAD.

I clipped this top panel off, then threw the letter out unread. It's cute and funny, but there are better, more tried-and-true, honest ways of earning welcome guest status for your sales letter. Gimmicks too often fail. Saying something of genuine importance and interest to the recipient usually succeeds.

Say it with a headline.

Yes, I am well aware that advertising has headlines, and letters generally do not. However, successful sales letters do. It can go above the salutation or between the salutation and the body copy. It can be typeset in big, bold type while the rest of the letter has a typewritten look. Or it can be put in a "Johnson box," a device presumably named after an inventor named Johnson, which looks like the one in Exhibit #8.

What your headline says and how it says it are absolutely critical. You might compare it to the door-to-door salesperson wedging a foot in the door, buying just enough time to deliver one or two sentences that will melt resistance, create interest, and elevate his or her status from annoying pest to welcome guest. You've got just about the same length of time, the same opportunity.

This book is not all about headlines, though an entire book certainly could be written about them. Instead, I've decided to give you some fill-in-the-blank headline structures that consistently and continually prove effective and successful. Many of these example headlines are classics from very successful books, advertisements, sales letters, and brochures, obtained from a number of research sources. Some are from my own sales letters. Some were created for this book.

Exhibit #8

September 12, 2005

Mr. Horace Buyer
President
ACME Co.
123 Business Street
City, State, Zip

Dear Mr. Buyer:

* * * * * * * * * * * * * * * * * *

Your headline goes here.

* * * * * * * * * * * * * * * * * * *

Body copy begins here and continues normal letter format.

Fill-in-the-Blank Headlines with Examples

THEY DIDN'T THINK I COULD _____ , BUT I DID.

This headline works well for many reasons, including our natural tendency to root for the underdog. We're fascinated by stories of people who overcome great obstacles and ridicule to achieve success. When this headline refers to something you have thought about doing, but talked yourself out of, you'll want to know if the successful person shared your doubt or fear or handicap.

Examples:

- They Laughed When I Sat Down At The Piano—But Not When I Started To Play!
- They Grinned When The Waiter Spoke To Me In French—But Their Laughter Changed To Amazement At My Reply!

WHO ELSE WANTS _____ ?

I like this type of headline because of its strong implication that a lot of other people know something that the reader doesn't.

Examples:

- Who Else Wants A Screen-Star Figure?
- Who Else Needs An Extra Hour Every Day?

HOW _____ MADE ME _____ .

This headline introduces a first-person story. People love stories, and are remarkably interested in other people. This headline structure seems to work best with dramatic differences.

Examples:

- How A "Fool Stunt" Made Me A Star Salesman.
- How A Simple Idea Made Me "Plant Manager Of The Year."
- How Relocating To Tennessee Saved Our Company One Million Dollars A Year.

ARE YOU _____?

The question headline is used to grab attention by challenging, provoking, or arousing curiosity.

Examples:

- Are You Ashamed Of The Smells In Your House?
- Are You Prepared For The Japanese Invasion Of Your Industry?

HOW I _____.

Very much like *How* _____ *Made Me* _____, this headline introduces a first-person story. The strength of the benefit at the end, obviously, controls its success.

Examples:

- How I Raised Myself From Failure To Success In Selling.
- How I Retired At Age 40—With A Guaranteed Income For Life.
- How I Turned A Troubled Company Into A Personal Fortune.

HOW TO _____.

This is a simple, straightforward headline structure that works with any desirable benefit. "How to" are two of the most powerful words you can use in a headline.

Examples:

- How To Collect From Social Security At Any Age.
- How To Win Friends And Influence People.
- How To Improve Telemarketers' Productivity—For Just $19.95.

A variation on this headline is to precede it with a specific "flag," a phrase calling for the attention of a particular person.

Examples:

- For The Executive With Work Left Over Every Day: How To Delegate Without Worry.
- For Busy Doctors: How To Educate New Patients In Half The Time.
- Stock Market Investors—How To Predict Short-Term Surges And Slumps.

IF YOU ARE _____, YOU CAN _____.

This is a creative twist on the "flagging" technique shown above, a way to make the headline specific to the intended reader.

Examples:

- If You Are A Nondrinker, You Can Save 20% On Life Insurance.
- If You Are A Football Expert, You Could Win $50,000.00 Next Weekend.
- If Your Firm Uses "Temporaries," You Might Qualify For $1,000.00 In Free Services.

SECRETS OF _____.

The word "secrets" works well in headlines.

Examples:

- Secrets Of A Madison Ave. Maverick—"Contrarian Advertising."
- Secrets Of Four Champion Golfers.

THOUSANDS (HUNDREDS, MILLIONS) NOW _____ EVEN THOUGH THEY _____.

This is a "plural" version of the very first structure demonstrated in this collection of winning headlines.

Examples:

- Thousands Now Play Even Though They Have "Clumsy Fingers."
- Two Million People Owe Their Health To This Idea Even Though They Laughed At It.
- 138,000 Members Of Your Profession Receive A Check From Us Every Month Even Though They Once Threw This Letter Into The Wastebasket.

WARNING: _____.

"Warning" is a powerful, attention-getting word, and can usually work for a headline tied to any sales letter using a problem-solution copy theme.

Examples:

- Warning: Two-Thirds Of The Middle Managers In Your Industry Will Lose Their Jobs In The Next 36 Months.
- Warning: Your "Corporate Shield" May Be Made Of Tissue Paper—9 Ways You Can Be Held Personally Liable For Your Business's Debts, Losses, Or Lawsuits.

GIVE ME _____ AND I'LL _____.

This structure simplifies the gist of any sales message: a promise. It truly telegraphs your offer, and if your offer is clear and good, this may be your best strategy.

Examples:

- Give Me 5 Days And I'll Give You A Magnetic Personality.
- Give Me Just 1 Hour A Day And I'll Have You Speaking French Like "Pierre" In One Month.
- Give Me A Chance To Ask Seven Questions And I'll Prove You Are Wasting A Small Fortune On Your Advertising.

_____ WAYS TO _____.

This is just the "how to" headline enhanced with an intriguing specific number.

Examples:

- 101 Ways To Increase New Patient Flow.
- 17 Ways To Slash Your Equipment Maintenance Costs.

Mention a Celebrity, Grab Attention

We live in a celebrity-obsessed culture, and even a brief mention of one can add attention-getting punch to an ad or sales letter.

My Gold/VIP Member Dr. Barry Lycka in Edmonton, Alberta, Canada, does this often, and cleverly. In a successful ad and direct-mail piece used to promote a seminar for prospective cosmetic procedure patients, he worked Oprah into the first sentence:

"If you have watched Oprah or the 6 o'clock news and wondered where you can get the latest cosmetic surgery done, you need look no further . . ."

Later, referring to a new line of cosmetic products available at his spa, Dr. Lycka wrote:

". . . the official makeup of the 75th Annual Academy Awards. It is used by Geena Davis, Holly Hunter, Jane Seymour and Paris Hilton, to name a few."

Many marketers have opportunities to connect celebrity name-dropping with their products or services and foolishly fail to do so. For years, I've urged chiropractors to name the many famous athletes who, in different interviews and news articles, have credited chiropractic care with keeping them fit. Few doctors do this. I'm involved in harness racing, and it pains me that the many celebrities who own these racehorses and love this sport are never mentioned by the United States Trotting Association or the racetracks in promotions to the public. Almost every client I work with has ways to link to celebrity. You probably do too!

Dr. Lycka, incidentally, helps other doctors with their practice promotion, advertising, patient education, even development of spa businesses—so you can be sure he'll get them using celebrity name-dropping!

Tips for Mailing to Executives and Business Owners

I believe that you have to give extra concern to your letter's image when preparing mailings to executives and business owners. These people respect and generally prefer to do business with successful merchants. Remember, too, that there are intermediaries to be dealt with: receptionists and assistants who may have the option of discarding or passing along your letter. For these reasons, I suggest that you follow these guidelines:

1. Use superior quality paper and envelopes—something with a texture or watermark.
2. Avoid stuffing many advertising enclosures in the envelope. One good approach is to put your brochures, order forms, and other essential pieces inside a second sealed package, enclosed in the main envelope with your sales letter. This presents a neat, businesslike appearance and draws attention to your sales letter.
3. Incorporate prestige appeals in your sales letter with words such as:

alternative	ownership preferred
association	prominent
attractive	select
charter member	superior
exceptional	uncompromising
exclusive	worthwhile
individual membership	yield

You can also incorporate prestige in your enclosures; plastic membership cards work well.

Speaking of "Grabbing" Attention

There is a direct-mail term, "grabber," that refers to some object attached to the sales letter, usually on the first page, or stuffed in with the letter, to grab the recipient's attention. This can be a simple thing, such as a penny or piece of foreign currency or tea bag stapled to the letter, or it can be a much more elaborate gimmick and item. In many cases, a multidimensional object is used to intentionally make the envelope "lumpy," to arouse the curiosity of the recipient. I love using such grabbers and urge all of my clients to do so.

In a recent mailing for my client Rory Fatt of Restaurant Marketing Systems, we sent the sales letter with a miniature aluminum trash can that had a little bag of peanuts inside. The letter was "from" a squirrel, that accused the nonresponsive prospect of being "nuts." We sent the trash can to dramatize the fact that not responding was the same as throwing $65,000.00 into the trash. This was a successful campaign for many reasons. But think about it: If somebody sends you a trash can full of peanuts, aren't you going to want to know why? That means you'll read the letter!

The real genius at sourcing and matching great grabbers and objects with direct-mail campaigns is Mitch Carson, who provides these items through his company, Impact Products, and teaches these strategies with hundreds of examples in his G.E.N.I.U.S. direct-mail system speeches, seminars, and tele-seminars.

Resource!

You can get more great case history examples, grabber ideas, and product sources from Mitch Carson at *www.impactproducts. net*. Mitch is also a frequent contributor to my monthly *No B.S. Marketing Letter*. You can get a free 3-month subscription at *www.Ultimate-Sales-Letter.com*.

Here's a great case history example from Mitch:

"The message in a bottle has been a big winner when we've used it to increase trade show traffic. For example, the National Academy of Sports Medicine wanted to mail something unusual that would grab attention and bring people to its trade show booth. We came up with a "treasure map" printed on parchment paper with burned edges, with an invitation printed on one side, the map to the booth on the other side. This was rolled up to go into the bottle. The same bottle also contained a small compass with the NASM logo, a magnifying glass (to read the map with), and a highlighter pen, also logo imprinted (to mark the map with). The bottle mailed with a label and postage on it, so you could see the objects inside. How could you *not* pay attention to this?"

The result: a 75 percent increase in targeted traffic, compared to previous years' shows. This is the kind of innovative thinking you need to invest in order to get your message read!

Tips for Mailing to the Mass Market

Bear in mind the attention span of the television generation: it is very short! Without a car chase, explosion, or gunfight every 10 seconds or so, the viewer may well click the remote control unit and move on. That conditioned impatience carries over to your sales letters, as well. You've got to reach out and grab the reader where he or she lives—immediately—then do it again and again and again. One or two sentences of less-than-compelling interest, and your reader will abandon you.

Involvement devices can help you grab and hold attention. Did you ever notice how Publishers Clearinghouse has you tearing out little stamps and pasting them onto the order card? Rub-off cards, tokens, stickers, and similar devices get the reader involved with the mailing.

You should also remember that color is virtually essential in consumer mailings. A number of bright, differently colored pieces are beneficial, as is color photography.

Tips for Mailings to Sell Products Directly

When you want the reader to make a decision to buy this item now—not commit to some intangible service or complicated agreement—you must follow several important guidelines:

1. Use testimonials from happy users of the product; these will do more than anything else to increase sales.
2. Remember that photographs outperform drawings and illustrations.
3. Prove that the product is easy to use. This may be done with copy, photographs, or testimonials—but it must be done!

Tips for Mailings to Sell Professional Services

Credibility is critical here. Descriptive statements of fact (such as number of years in business, number of clients served, sample client lists, and so on) can all be of tremendous value.

However, "believability" is even more important than "credibility."

The facts about your business, such as years in business, clients served, proprietary methods, and so on are important, but not nearly as persuasive as what clients have to say about their real-life experiences with you, benefits realized, and skepticism erased.

Facts and credibility only support persuasion.

Consider offering a free initial consultation or a free package of informative literature; this may break down barriers of skepticism and mistrust. Answer the question: Why should the reader bother? Similarly, you should work at making the intangible benefits of your product tangible. This can be accomplished with before/after photographs, slice-of-life stories, case histories, or other examples. Demonstrate the value!

Postcards Can Produce Big Profits, Too

As general rules, I like using postcards when mailing to consumers (but not business-to-business, where there are gatekeepers ruthlessly trashing B-pile mail); for simple offers; and when communicating with people with whom a relationship is established (rather than with new prospects). But rules are made to be broken!

One of my Platinum Members, Dr. Chris Brady, who markets a "Rich Dentist/Poor Dentist" seminar and a $70,000.00 coaching program, has had good success with a large fold-out self-mailer that mails flat, not in an envelope (Exhibit #9). Another variation of this is what I call the road-map postcard. It also has 8½" × 11" surfaces, but is not staple-bound like Dr. Brady's. It is one big sheet, folded down to mail flat, that unfolded provides 8 full pages for copy.

Exhibit #9

Exhibit #9 (continued)

It's my 20th year in Dentistry & I'm Celebrating All Across America For the Entire Year of 2004 Beginning with a....

FREE SEMINAR!

"Totally FREE (& GUARANTEED) Practice Upgrade Seminar"

Exclusively for Dentists Quality and Their Teams

Over the last decade, Doctor Chris Brady has taught principles and concepts that have changed the lives of literally tens of thousands of people. Doctor Brady is Founder and President of The Brady Group headquartered in Colorado Springs, Colorado. He has spoken to groups and practices all over the United States, and Brady members can be found from coast to coast. He still practices cosmetic and restorative dentistry to this day. Doctor Brady's numerous articles can be found in various publications such as Dental Economics and Contemporary Dental Aesthetics, and sits on the Editorial Board at Dentist's Money Digest.

A renowned lecturer, Dr. Brady was the keynote speaker at the 2003 American Academy of Cosmetic Dentistry meeting in Orlando. He was voted one of the top speakers at that seminar! He loves teaching essential skills of leadership, management, and communication to doctors which enables them to build the practice they have only dreamed about. He shares his secrets and techniques to lower overhead, increase vacation time, lower stress, increase case acceptance, reduce or eliminate dental insurance, significantly increase doctor's net income, and much much more!

Exhibit #9 (continued)

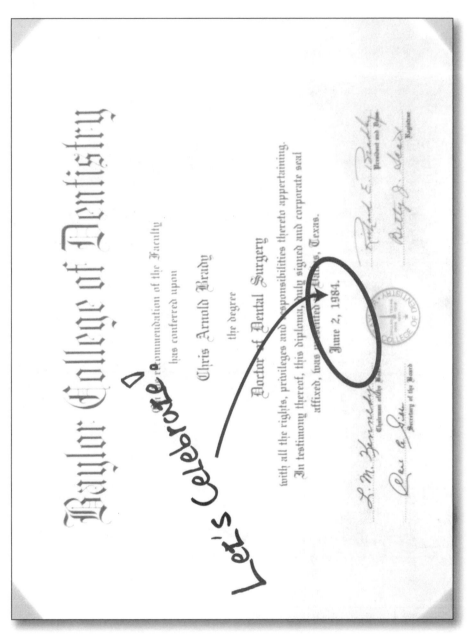

Exhibit #9 (continued)

Still Stuck In The 80's?

Remember When...

1. In 1984, Posterior composites were just starting to gain some acceptance.
2. In 1984, prepping veneers required no (or very little) reduction of tooth structure.
3. In 1984, the Caridex machine made a very brief appearance with its claim to dissolve decay.
4. In 1984, curing and etching took at least 60 seconds and etching dentin "killed" teeth.
5. In 1984, calcium hydroxide, was a staple in every office - gloves and masks were NOT!
6. In 1984, Computer imaging was done on a 286 computer.
7. In 1984, the AACD was just getting started and LVI didn't exist.

Is Your Business Costing You?

1. Are you still accepting insurance assignment?
2. Are you still sending monthly statements?
3. Do you still think that selling dentistry requires educating the patient and telling them what they need?
4. Are you a member of the 'crown of the year club'?
5. Do you still think you have to work more hours in order to make more money?
6. Do you still think that getting more new patients is the key to making more money?
7. Are you well on your way to creating a "dental superstore" in an attempt to be all things to all people?

Is Your Business Performance Decades Behind?

As you probably know, the Brady Group has been around for quite some time - over 10 years. During that time, we have seen thousands of practices and have developed a stellar reputation for helping top notch practices achieve their dreams. Over the past 20 years, I have personally learned a lot about the state of the industry all across America - and I am disappointed. I am disappointed that the majority of dentists are not really getting what they want from their practices. They just aren't getting the results that allow them to run a successful practice without giving up their personal and family lives.

So I was thinking, "How can I repay this great profession we are all engaged in?" One of my staff members suggested I give away a series of free seminars as a way of saying 'thanks for a great 20 years.' At first I thought it was a dumb idea - but it has started to grow on me and now I have committed to doing it - nationwide. (My accountant thinks I'm stupid for spending all this time and money sharing what I have learned and how I have helped other colleagues - but it's my time and my money and I can do with it what I want - and this gives me much satisfaction to see practices change & improve while doctors and their teams catch this vision of what their practices can be like).

Now, you may be thinking, "How can a free seminar be worth going to? We all know you 'get what you pay for!' There's got to be a catch. Maybe all the doors will have automatic locks on them and no one will be allowed to leave until they buy something. Or maybe this will be an all day 'sales job' and I won't really get anything from attending." In truth - I appreciate the skepticism - it tells me you're serious about your practice. None of these concerns are true. In fact, I'm offering a guarantee... a guarantee of $5,000. This is a one of a kind guarantee you will never see at any other seminar!

Take a look at just a few of the topics we will be covering,

1. Learn how to fix the high gross, low net problem.
2. Increasing case acceptance.
3. Lowering stress on both doctors and their teams.
4. How to eliminate the insurance objection.
5. Learn the mistakes 99% of all dentists make that are costing them dearly.
6. Learn why what you're experiencing is a result of bad systems - not a lack of effort.

Exhibit #9 (continued)

How can you go wrong with a free seminar and a free lunch backed by a $5,000 guarantee?

So, are you tired of paying for expensive seminars only to be disappointed in the ROI? Are you tired of the kind of seminar that leaves you feeling good for a while, only to find that there really wasn't an impact to your bottom line. Are you tired of the seminar that simply deposits more notes in a binder to collect dust? Are you tired of having to wonder, "Will this seminar be worth the money?" If this sounds like you, then this seminar is what you have been looking for.

We will not be focusing on the latest, whiz bang equipment available, hoping to impress patients with laser & digital doohickeys. We won't focus on how to create a relaxing, 'spa' atmosphere in order to attract patients. You already know that the gadgets and techniques are not the most important piece of the puzzle in putting together a truly great practice. What we will focus on is the most important aspect of a successful dental practice - the 'software.' I'm not talking about the newest release of Dental Suite 4.0 - I'm talking about the business processes & techniques that will allow you to effectively run and manage your practice.

If you don't get enough solid, practical, full of meat information from this FREE seminar to increase your income by at least 10%, I'll pay you $5,000.

"The Brady Group program has organized a practice philosophy and system that has me working fewer hours, enjoying dentistry more, and significantly increasing my net profit."

-Ronald Van Wechel, D.D.S., Denver, CO

"No more emergencies! No more fear of my beeper ruining my personal time. The phone only rings when someone wants non-crisis dentistry!"

-Pamela Gates, D.D.S., Denver, CO

Here's what we offer our dentists,

- More time off to spend with family & friends.
- 6 weeks of vacation for doctors and their teams.
- More fun and satisfaction by doing the kind of dentistry you most enjoy.
- More money (if you do what you enjoy you will be rewarded with greater financial success).
- Lower accounts receivable (some of our doctors carry no accounts receivable whatsoever!).
- Bigger cases and more large cosmetic cases.
- Lover overhead.
- Increased diagnosis for more long term, higher quality dentistry.
- Less stress.
- Easier, quicker resolution to staff issues.

For Your Success,

Dr. Chris Brady President, Brady Group

Seating Is Limited - Call for Reservations Today
(214) 212-4595

Exhibit #9 (continued)

Exhibit #9 (continued)

↱ *Tear to Fax*   A FREE Seminar with a $5,000 Guarantee?

Yes, Count Me In!

⬭ **I do want to increase the successfulness of my practice! Definitely** *reserve a seat for me in this intensive, high impact session which is guaranteed to put money in my pocket and free time in my hands.*

⬭ **I understand that the $5,000 Guarantee** *requires that I attend, pay attention, listen, and implement the many ways I can improve my bottom line.*

⬭ **By bringing my staff,** *I realize I will not have to try and gain their "buy-in" or convince them of the opportunity in front of me to increase the overall health of my business.*

2004
Seminar Schedule
Mark Your Seminar Selection

◯ *Dallas, TX* **Aug 26** 3:00 PM - 9:00 PM
◯ *Houston, TX* **Aug 27** 9:00 AM - 4:00 PM
◯ *Denver, CO* **Sep 23** 93:00 PM - 9:00 PM
◯ *Denver, CO* **Sep 24** 9:00 AM - 4:00 PM
◯ *Houston, TX* **Sep 30** 3:00 PM - 9:00 PM
◯ *Dallas, TX* **Oct 1** 9:00 AM - 4:00 PM
◯ *Salt Lake City, UT* **Oct 14** 3:00 PM - 9:00 PM
◯ *Salt Lake City, UT* **Oct 15** 9:00 AM - 3:00 PM

Lunch or Dinner is On Me!

This event will change the way you live and work.
Seating Is Limited

Sign Me Up!
I am providing my credit card information for a refundable deposit to secure my seat in this session. My card will not be charged the $75 administration fee *unless* I fail to attend.

Of Course I Will Bring My Staff!
By bringing my staff I will be able to jump start my entire team. In addition to myself, please reserve seating for the following:

_____
_____
_____

If the doctor does not attend, the Staff Registration Fee is: $649
This Fee Is Waived If The Primary Doctor Attends

Here's My Billing Information:

Card Number:_____ Expires:_____
Name (exactly as it appears on the card) _____
Authorized Signature_____

My Registration Information:

Name:_____
Company:_____
Address:_____
_____
State:_____ Zip:_____
Phone:(____) _____ Fax:(____) _____
E-Mail:_____

Call for Reservations Today
(800) 396-5669 or
FAX Registration Form to:
(972) 264-5484
Please make a copy of this form to facilitate faxing in your registration.

Exhibit #9 (concluded)

For many purposes, a less elaborate, slightly oversized postcard is sufficient. Bill Glazer uses this format a lot for his retail stores. (See examples of this format in the free 12-Week Ultimate Sales Letter course delivered by e-mail, at *www.Ultimate-Sales-Letter.com*.)

Resource!

You can find premade photographic image postcards with fill-in-the-blank templates for a variety of promotional purposes, with the copy written by me, available for your instant use at *www.petetheprinter.com*.

A "Tricky" Direct-Mail Piece That Often Out-Performs Sales Letters

In print advertising, there is a format called an "advertorial," which refers to an ad made to look like editorial content; like an article. There's a good example of one of these in this book's companion, *The Ultimate Marketing Plan*—look for Bill Glazer's "sprinkler malfunction" ad. These advertorials often outperform ads that look like ads for the same product or service. One of the big reasons is simply readership. People buy newspapers and magazines for articles more than for ads, and are much more likely to read the articles than the ads. So the ad that masquerades as an article has a better opportunity to get a greater number of readers involved.

In direct mail, the advertorial is replicated as a tear-sheet mailing. Many of these are so successful that such pieces are mailed in the millions, so you've probably received at least a few every year. The mailing piece may mimic a newspaper or magazine. Let's use the newspaper as example. What actually arrives in the envelope is a piece that's the size of a newspaper page, printed on a newsprint type of paper, and formatted like a news article or advertorial. Sometimes innocuous stock quotes or other, unrelated articles are printed on the back, and sometimes one side has jagged edges as if torn out of a newspaper, to further the illusion. A little sticky note is stuck on the folded newspaper page, with a handwritten message such as: "Thought you'd want to see this too—J." Everybody knows people with "J" as their first initial. John, Jerry, Janice. They think somebody they know has torn this out and sent it to them. They read it. Now it has a chance.

Let's compare response rates for 100 standard sales letters and 100 tear-sheet mailings. An ordinary sales letter might start out with only 10 percent of recipients reading it, but the tear sheet may start with 30 percent or 40 percent or 50 percent reading it. If half of all tear-sheet recipients read the piece, that'd be 50 readers. If only 10 percent of those actually reading respond to the piece, that would be 5 responses out of 100 pieces mailed ($50 \times 10\% = 5$). To produce 5 responses, the ordinary sales letter would have to get 50 percent of its readers to respond!

One of the biggest users of tear-sheet mailers is a newsletter called the *American Speaker*. It uses magazine tear sheets rather than those from newspapers. According to an article in the *Washington Post*, this publisher, Georgetown Publishing, sends out as many as 5 million of these pieces each year.

Probably the person who knows the most about these, because his company produces and mails them for so many different marketers, is Craig Dickhout at Think Ink. Craig says he has coordinated the production and mailing of more than 300 million of these tear-sheet mailings! His company has produced the mailings for Georgetown Publishing as well as Met-RX, Guthy-Renker, and Health Laboratories, to name a few. A lot of the use is by companies in the seminar, home-study course, and newsletter businesses and by diet, nutrition, and health-product direct marketers, which mail large quantities to national lists. However, I've had clients in many other, diverse businesses who use these kinds of mailings, both locally and nationally.

Craig points out:

"All the tiny little nuances of these pieces, and the envelopes they are mailed in, are critically important. The writing on the sticky note must appear real and authentic, not mass printed. The tear sheet must be typeset, formatted, and made to appear as an article from a credible publication, without, of course, using any actual publication's name or copyright and trademark protected items. The envelope must be anonymous and be personalized in a way that looks truly personalized."

This works so well that there are legal considerations. Today, the big users put "Advertisement" in small print, on both the sticky note and the tear sheet. As far as anyone can tell, it's made no difference. If you are going to use this approach, you may want to work with a printer and mailing house who are thoroughly familiar with its use and the laws governing its use. If you want to get information from Craig, you can fax him at Think Ink, at 714-374-7071.

I have a final tip about this and any other type of mailing that "sneaks up" and "tricks" the recipient into reading it: you will annoy some people. Some people resent being tricked. If you are operating in a tiny or limited market in which people talk to each other a lot, you may want to be especially cautious about this. However, the effectiveness often outweighs the annoyance factor. Personally, I'm of the gotta-break-a-few-eggs-to-make-an-omelet school. In general, the best way to minimize annoyance and maximize response is to make certain you are mailing your promotion to targeted prospects or customers who will have a high degree of interest in it once motivated to read it.

Beat the Price Bugaboo

Although any good sales pro will admit that price is very rarely the determining factor in a buying decision, that same pro will tell you that, mishandled, price can put the brakes on a sale before it even gets going.

The sales letter writer has to decide, before actually writing the letter, how to present price and what strategies to use in minimizing the impact of price. Certainly, if price is a key issue in your business, you'll want to minimize it to whatever degree possible in the mind of your letter recipient. Here, then, are the best price minimizers I know.

Compare Apples to Oranges

There's no law that says you have to stick with logical, apples-to-apples comparisons. You are much better off with a comparison that confuses the price issue.

In a publishing/mail-order company that I ran for five years, we sold specialized, high-priced audiocassette courses to dentists and chiropractors. The going price for a spoken-word, business-oriented audiocassette was—and still is—about $10.00. Most of the companies in this business price a six-cassette album at $49.95 to $69.95—$8.33 to $11.66 per tape. Our single programs, however, averaged out to at least $16.58 and as much as $23.00 per tape. The last thing we wanted to do was compare the prices of our apples and their apples! Instead, we compared the prices of our cassette programs to the costs of attending the seminars on which the tapes were based. For example: "... to attend the Practice Promotion Seminar just one time would cost you at least $195.00 as an enrollment fee, plus travel, lodging overnight, and the time away from your practice or your family—certainly several hundred dollars or more. But when you get this same important information in cassette form, you can listen and learn at your convenience, share with associates and staff members, and pay only $95.00."

I continue to use this very same cassettes-to-seminars, apples-to-oranges comparison today, in sales letter after sales letter, for more than a dozen different clients in the publishing industry, proving the reliability of the strategy. Whatever your product, service, or offer, you need to look for a way to make easy, direct-price comparison difficult.

My Platinum Member Yanik Silver called my attention to a great apples/oranges example from the online world. An e-book titled *Get Fit While You Sit* is sold for $19.00 to $29.00 at *www.GetFitWhileYouSit.com*. Instead of comparing this to other fitness books or videos, Yanik has used copy comparing it to an expensive piece of fitness equipment, a gym membership, and hiring a personal trainer. As you can see when you visit this site and study the copy, in each case he's done the math for them, and done his best to build the value through these comparisons, so that when he finally reveals the price, it feels insignificant. One of the most important things about this example is that he's added up these comparative costs for the prospect. He hasn't asked them to do the selling work for him.

_____ **Resource!** _____

Yanik Silver has a great Web site to help sales letter writers: *www. InstantSalesLetter.com*. Yanik also is a featured monthly contributor to my *No B.S. Marketing Letter*. You can get a free 3-month subscription at *www.Ultimate-Sales-Letter.com*.

Sell Bulk

People do equate value with bulk. One of the very first sales letters for an offer of books was for the Harvard Classics, and it proudly proclaimed its bulk: "Dr. Elliott's Five-Foot Shelf Of Books." I shamelessly copied this idea for a client, with this line: "These three information-packed books weigh over thirteen pounds and cost nearly twenty dollars just to ship to your door!"

One of my clients, a Platinum-level Glazer-Kennedy Inner Circle Member, very recently emphasized this idea in one of his sales letters, saying: "... and you'd better go down to Wal-Mart and buy the biggest bookshelf you can buy, for the huge truckload of moneymaking information in books, manuals, and courses that I'm going to give you, free, when ..."

If you are selling an information product like books, cassettes, or subscriptions, remember that one way to convey bulk is with a list of the 1,001 (or some other huge, specific number) pieces of information contained in your product. You'll see the leaders in this field, including *Boardroom Reports* and Rodale Press, do this repeatedly.

If you are selling some other type of product, the same principle applies. For example, if we were writing a sales letter for an ordinary apple, instead of just saying that "an apple a day keeps the doctor away," we might list every vitamin and mineral provided by the apple, then list every health benefit delivered by each of those vitamins and minerals. We might then show the huge bulk of other foods you'd have to consume to get those same nutrients and benefits—all to turn that little apple into a huge "bulk" of benefits and value.

Discuss the Price Paid to Develop the Offer

Is this relevant to the consumer? Maybe not, but that doesn't prevent you from making it relevant.

Consider the difference between these two ways of telling you about a piece of automated industrial equipment:

VERSION #1

It automatically selects the right amount of material, fills the bag, seals it, and stacks it in the carton. It gets it right every time. And it is an extraordinarily durable system, good for tens of thousands of repetitions without needing maintenance.

VERSION #2

Our company recruited a brain trust of eight of the very best, most knowledgeable robotics engineers in industry today to design this system. No expense was spared in obtaining the services of these experts. The prototype system was run over six months of laboratory tests at a cost of over one million dollars before ever being placed in an actual working environment. In the ultimate test, we put it through 15,000 repetitions, and it performed perfectly and never needed even a minute of downtime for maintenance. You can count on this system to select the right amount of material every time, fill the bag, seal it, and stack it in the carton without error. With over three million dollars' worth of research and quality control backing you up, you'll finally have at least one piece of equipment working for you that is as reliable as God's sunrise.

Both copy versions describe the same machine and the exact same benefits. But the second version builds value.

Make the Parts Worth More than the Whole

Have you ever seen the "pitchmen" at the state or county fair, with crowds gathered around them, selling things like slicer-dicers, sets of kitchen knives, or similar gadgets? These people are artistic masters at building high perceived value for each little doodad, each attachment, each part, so that when it's all added up it is much, much more than the price of the whole unit. The "value overage" in such presentations is overwhelming. This same strategy works in more sophisticated settings, too.

Consider the example shown in Exhibit #10.

Conceal the Price

This is a strategy being used in print ads, sales letters, and even television commercials, for a variety of consumer-product, book, and subscription offers. These marketers present prices like this: "Just three small monthly installments of $11.95 charged to your credit card."

While this has taken hold as a norm for the entire direct-response industry only in the past handful of years, the approach is not really much of an innovation; the automobile industry has been using it for some time. I just got a sales letter from a local Cadillac dealership about its annual used car sale; the letter included an 8½" × 11" list of all the cars, arranged by brand, model, color, options, and stock number. The cars were grouped into "payment categories"—one list at $199.00 per month, one at $249.00 per month, another at $399.00 per month.

Recently I've had success, with both consumer and business-to-business marketing clients, in getting higher prices by disguising them in payments. For example, in one direct test, there was absolutely no difference in the number of sales generated by "$39.95" vs. "2 payments of $19.95" vs. "3 payments of $19.95." The third option is a higher price, but no difference! In a business-to-business situation, one piece of equipment, a $5,000.00 item, was sold in 4 payments of $1,250.00. I helped the client develop an upgraded, premium version of the same product that sold for $7,000.00, but was presented as "8 payments of $875.00." The higher-priced item has a lower monthly payment than the lower-priced item does—and 72 percent of the buyers opted for this lower monthly payment choice!

Exhibit #10

The typical doctor saves thousands of dollars with our Full-Service System Concept for practice promotion and management. Consider the value of everything you get as a System Client:

6 SEMINARS DURING THE 24-MONTH CONTRACT

Each 2-day Seminar focuses on a different aspect of practice success: Advertising, Referrals, Money Management, and much more. Each Seminar features appropriate, expert guest lecturers as well as our Team Trainers. If you sought out individually offered seminars covering these same topic areas, you would pay at least $195 to as much as $395 for each one. So this is at least a $1,200 value.

THE 24-MONTH MARKETING KIT

24 newspaper ads, 24 different patient newsletters, 24 different seasonal referral stimulation letter campaigns, 24 different in-office hand-outs . . . all designed by our own advertising experts, an advisory group of 10 successful doctors, and Dr. Bill Whosis himself. We've priced this—the typical ad agency would charge more than $10,000.00 to create all of this for you from scratch! Even if you did it yourself, and just hired freelancers to do the typesetting, illustrations, and layout work, you'd spend at least $3,000.00, probably more.

TAPE-OF-THE-MONTH CLUB

Each month you'll receive a new audiocassette for your own use, and a new videocassette with four Staff Meeting Starter Sessions on it. Just at prevailing prices for general-interest audio and video materials, this is nearly a $1,000 value. Of course, this specialized practice-building information is worth much more!

If you add up all of this, you've got at least $5,200.00 in "hard value"—in reality, a lot more—but your entire 24-month fee is only $3,895.00! And that's not all! When you join us within the next 60 days . . . before the end of this calendar year . . . you receive three very special, valuable bonus gifts and services ABSOLUTELY FREE!

First, a monthly review of your statistics and finances by our team of accountants, financial planners, and doctors, followed by a one-page Report of Findings and Recommendations. Second, our famous "How to Build Community Prominence" Self-Study Course with 6 audiotapes, 1 videotape, and a 200-page manual . . . including interviews with seven very successful doctors from different parts of the country about their public relations successes. And, third, an opportunity to compete in our "Most Improved Doctor of the Year" competition, for an expense-paid Hawaiian vacation and exciting runner-up prizes.

Three Letter Formulas That Let You Transcend Price Questions

Now let's look at three of the most effective copywriting formulas you can use to overcome a reader's hesitation on the issue of price (and on many other issues as well). These formulas relate to the price question because they get the reader to focus on something other than how much money he is going to spend—and isn't that your objective?

The formulas are easy to understand, adaptable to many business situations, and—most important—they work.

FORMULA #1

Problem-Agitation-Solution

When you understand that people are more likely to act to avoid pain than to get gain, you'll understand how incredibly powerful this first formula is. I have used this basic formula to structure supereffective sales presentations for live salespeople in every imaginable business, from security systems to skin-care products. I've used it for more than 136 different industries, and not only for sales letters, but also for salespeople. It may be *the* most reliable sales formula ever invented.

The first step is to define the customer's problem. You may be writing about a problem they know they have or about a problem they don't know they have—it matters very little, because a good sales letter avoids assuming knowledge on the part of the recipient. So the letter sets forth the problem in clear, straightforward terms. Here you need to say only enough to elicit agreement. For a letter promoting a tax-strategies course for small business owners, this part of the letter can be very brief:

> You, the small business owner, are already the government's #1 tax target. Every time you look at your mail, there's another tax form

demanding your attention and your money. Now you will also pay the highest price for the new tax reform—unless you discover a few secrets normally used only by "the big guys" to fight back!

If you're presenting a more complex problem, you may need to say a great deal more and add proof to your premise. A client for whom I wrote a number of sales letters some years ago was a consultant on employee and deliveryman theft in retail businesses. Because most retailers (incorrectly and stubbornly) believe that their theft problems are with shoplifters rather than with their own employees, I had to take as much as half the letter to demonstrate with facts, statistics, case examples, and other credible information that their real problem was internal.

Once the problem is established, clearly and factually, it's time to inject emotion. This second step is agitation. That means we stir up the letter recipients' emotional responses to the problem. We tap their anger, resentment, guilt, embarrassment, fear—any and every applicable negative emotion. We want to whip them into a fervor! We want to make the problem larger than life, worse than death.

My sales-trainer friend, the famous (late) Cavett Robert, said that to sell life insurance or cemetery plots, you have to make your customer see the hearse backed up to the door. That may sound a little grisly, but it's true.

Here's agitation copy from a sales letter for a very ordinary product: shoes.

. . . but if you insist on just wearing any old pair of ordinary shoes, here's what you have to look forward to in your so-called golden years; fallen arches . . . intense lower back pain . . . extraordinary discomfort in golf or tennis shoes . . . even pain from just walking around a shopping mall! You'll be asking your friends to slow down so you can keep up. You'll be futilely soaking your feet at night like some old fuddy-duddy. You may even need pain pills just to get to sleep.

And here's agitation copy from one of the sales letters sent to CEOs of grocery-store chains by my theft-control expert:

The next time you look out the big picture window of your home at your beautiful, manicured lawn, think about this: a client of mine, the owner of 16 supermarkets, told me he was doing just that—looking happily out his window across his lawn at the half-million-dollar home diagonally across the street, where his new neighbors were moving in. Imagine his shock when he realized that his new neighbor was the driver of the soft-drink delivery truck that serviced his supermarkets! Yes, that deliveryman was paying for his half-million-dollar home with money from the goods he had stolen from my client's supermarkets.

You worked hard to build up your business. The employees and vendors stealing from you have no capital investment in stores, no bank loans to worry about, no tax forms to fill out. You've earned your success and they're stealing it from you, right under your nose! And if you refuse to see it, you are "the emperor with no clothes." In fact, they're laughing at you, right now, behind your back. I know. I was one of them. Long before I became a security consultant, I was a deliveryman-thief! I conspired with other deliverymen just like the ones who service your stores. I conspired with employees just like the ones working in your stores. And together we stole and stole and stole some more.

If you were the owner of a chain of stores, would that rattle your cage a little? (By the way, please note that everything I wrote about the expert—whose signature appeared on the above letter—was true.)

After you've clearly stated the problem, and after you've created tremendous agitation about the problem, you should have readers mentally wringing their hands, pacing the room, saying: "This has got to stop! I've got to do something about this! What can I do about this? If only there were an answer!" And that's right where you want them!

It's at that point, that crucial moment, that you whip out the solution. The third step is to unveil the solution, the answer—your product or services, and the accompanying benefits.

An example of a complete sales letter using this formula is shown as Exhibit #11.

FORMULA #2

Fortunetelling

Our fascination with those who predict the future never ends. One very savvy public relations agent told me: "The two keys to unlimited media attention and publicity are being predictive and being provocative." Who's going to win the Super Bowl this year? What will the stock market do next? When will the next earthquake occur? What will happen in the next millennium? And on and on and on.

John Naisbitt rose from obscurity to celebrity as a best-selling author, business guru, highly paid lecturer, consultant, and social commentator, all thanks to his predictive book *Megatrends*. More recently, economist Harry Dent traveled exactly the same path, achieving fame by predicting evolving trends. In corporate America, yet another example is Faith Popcorn.

Exhibit #11

Dear Computer Hater,

DO YOU HATE YOUR COMPUTER?

DO YOU OWN A COMPUTER THAT
WON'T DO WHAT YOU TELL IT TO DO?

ARE YOU AFRAID TO BUY A COMPUTER—
EVEN THOUGH YOU KNOW YOU NEED ONE?

ARE YOU CONFUSED BY COMPUTER-BABBLE?

In a recent survey taken by the Small Business Research Institute, over 74% of the small business owners who had purchased computers in the past 12 months felt they had been "ripped off" . . . lied to about what the computers would do for them; how easy they were to use; or the help and support available. Over 30% said their costly computers were now being used as typewriters or, worse, sitting in a corner gathering dust.

If you're in this group of frustrated, disappointed computer owners, you've literally flushed thousands, maybe tens of thousands of dollars right down the toilet!!! Is that how a savvy businessperson behaves? Of course not!

If you're afraid to "computerize" because of these problems— well, do successful businesspeople live in fear? Of course not.

We have the solution you need.

We're "PC SOLUTIONS," and here's what we'll do for you:

1. We will always talk with you in plain English. No computer-babble.

2. We will objectively analyze your needs "from scratch." We'll tell you what a computer system will and will not do for you.

Exhibit #11 (concluded)

---

3. If you already have computer equipment and software, we will:

   A. Evaluate it and help you understand it—quickly

   B. Make it work for you, if possible

   C. Teach your people how to use it

   D. If it's "wrong" for you, we'll do battle with whoever sold it to you to get it traded in, replaced or repaired

   E. If necessary, we'll modify it or add to it at the lowest cost possible

4. If you haven't purchased computers yet, we'll guide you in doing so . . . picking the right equipment and software for your needs. We do NOT sell computers or software. We're on your side!

Why suffer with unproductive computers, unhappy staff, anger, frustration? Call PC-SOLUTIONS today for a FREE, NO-OBLI-GATION 30-MINUTE CONSULTATION.

1-800-DISKJOY

To prove how evergreen this approach is, Exhibit #12, which promotes a "crisis investing" publication, appeared in the first edition of this book (1991). If you subscribe to investment newsletters, watch your mailbox for new sales letters promoting investment newsletters. You'll see sales letters today using exactly the same themes as this one did more than a decade ago.

This is as good a time as any to call your attention to that recurring theme: Good, solid, time-tested sales and sales letter strategies do not wear out or become obsolete. What worked in a sales letter in 1950 will still work in 2050, with only slight language modification.

Exhibit #12

ENCLOSED:
Doug Casey's new investment
predictions for 1987

JUST RELEASED FOR MARCH 1987

■ We are already in the beginning phases of the next Great Depression—which promises to be much worse than the last one! But this economic upheaval will provide spectacular opportunities—*profits of 500% to 1000%*—for shrewd investors *(see page 1)*.

■ A surprising list of global investment "hot spots" *(see page 5)*.

■ 3 best opportunities to make your million(s) in the second half of the '80s *(see page 3 inside)*.

■ Escalating problems in South Africa will trigger a price explosion in certain raw materials *(see page 1)*.

■ Suicide terrorists will soon be able to hold entire cities hostage—with undetectable nuclear mini-bombs. *Primary targets:* Wall Street, Silicon Valley and other key economic centers *(see page 4 inside)*.

■ A financial accident will spark the greatest bank panic since the Great Depression. (11 of today's *unsafest big financial institutions are named on page 4 inside)*

■ Higher interest rates will return. Bonds will be mauled *(see page 4)*.

■ Special recommendation concerning T-bills *(see page 4 inside)*.

■ **PLUS,** *a unique opportunity to get rich as a "white-collar" farmer. You could actually have the potential to run a portfolio of $10,000 into $150,000 within the next two years (see page 6 inside).*

Please turn over to page 1 for more details...

INVESTING IN CRISIS
P.O. Box 1464
Alexandria, VA 22313

BULK RATE
U.S. POSTAGE

402187

DAN S KENNEDY
PHOENIX, AZ 85020

Reprinted courtesy of Agora Publishing Co., Baltimore, Maryland.

FORMULA #3

Winners and Losers

Very early in my selling career, I was taught a "pitch" that reads/sounds something like this:

> Take any hundred people at the start of their working careers and follow them for 40 years until they reach retirement age, and here's what you'll find, according to the Social Security Administration: Only 1 will be wealthy; 4 will be financially secure; 5 will continue working, not because they want to but because they have to; 36 will be dead; and 54 will be dead broke—dependent on their meager Social Security checks, relatives, friends, even charity for a minimum standard of living. That's 5% successful, 95% unsuccessful.

That same basic comparison has been used to sell everything from life insurance and investments to real-estate-buying schemes and Amway distributorships. I have used it face-to-face, speaking from the platform and in print, thousands and thousands of times. It quickly gains attention, opens minds, and makes people think. Then, whatever it is you are selling is presented as the path to joining the 5% group, the big difference between the winners and the losers.

The reason I was taught this material and the reason it is used so widely, repetitively, and continuously is that it works. People understand it. It creates fear—fear of being in the 95% group. It creates motivation— motivation to be in the 5% group.

The *Wall Street Journal* has used variations of this theme in many of its sales letters over the years. One of its most successful sales letters tells the story of two college graduates—one successful, one not, with the difference being that one subscribes to the *Journal*.

Here's an example of the formula from a sales letter I wrote for a lawn and garden store back in the early 1970s:

Last spring, two neighbors reseeded their lawns. Now it's June.

One has a beautiful, lush, thick green lawn. As perfect as the best golf course in the country. A lawn to be proud of.

His neighbor, though, has a different lawn. With little brown patches. Uneven texture. Crabgrass and weeds fighting for territory.

What made the difference?

The letter goes on to tout the virtues of "lawn care counseling" from the store's owners, and a particular line of lawn care products and fertilizers. It will work just as well today (in the right geographic areas—the 'burbs) as it did almost 20 years ago. In fact, in 1998, I recycled it for a landscaping company's franchisees, and several have reported phenomenal results.

These three formulas can be used separately or combined in a single sales letter. At least one of them and probably all of them can work for your business.

Review Winning Copywriting Techniques and Tactics

I once flew across the country seated next to a grizzled, old-time direct-sales pro who told me about getting started during the tail end of the Great Depression, selling vacuum cleaners door to door. When the sales manager hired this fellow, he gave him a giant looseleaf notebook of 299 "sales techniques" to use in getting past the front door, demonstrating the vacuum, and closing the sale. He had to memorize and be tested on his knowledge of those techniques before going out into the field.

"How many of the two hundred and ninety-nine did you wind up using?" I asked him.

"Oh, I tried 'em all," he said, "but after thirty days in the trenches I was down to using the three or four that worked."

I've had similar experiences with copywriting. Early in my career, I assembled a reference library of literally hundreds of books about advertising, marketing, direct response, direct mail, mail order, and copywriting, each full of dozens of different techniques. I suppose I've tried hundreds of them. And, over the years, I've narrowed it down to a handful that work consistently and almost universally. So, consider this an enormously valuable shortcut. If you want to experiment, go ahead and do so, but if you simply want to be effective and efficient, then you can stick with just a few proven techniques. In fact, you can probably take care of all of your sales letter needs for years to come just with these few. Here they are.

TECHNIQUE #1: Intimidation

In person-to-person, professional selling, I very quickly learned the value of intimidation, and I consider Robert Ringer's best-selling book *Winning Through Intimidation* to be one of the most useful business books I've ever read. From that book and my own experiences, I learned that the hardest deal to make is the one you desperately need or really, really want to make. Somehow, the other person always senses that, and it scares him or her away. On the other hand, the easiest deal closings occur when you feel that you don't need them and really don't much care whether they come to fruition or not. This is called "taking a position," and it applies equally well to selling in print.

Here are some interesting ways to "take a position."

1. Limited Number Available

Mints, sellers of collectibles, and rare-coin dealers use this strategy with great effectiveness, but it's certainly not limited to them. Many times I've used copy like this for a limited-quantity offer:

> . . . if your response is received after our supply is exhausted, it will not be accepted and your check will be returned uncashed.

This is intimidating!

2. Most Will Buy

This technique relies on what is sometimes called the "bandwagon effect," creating the idea that a huge trend has developed, everybody is getting involved, and anyone who passes it up is, quite simply, an idiot. Here's an example of this kind of copy:

> . . . thousands have joined in the last 30 days. Only a small number of people have received this invitation, and we fully expect most of them to take immediate advantage of this amazing discount—so if our phone lines are busy when you call, please be patient and keep trying. We have added extra customer-service people to handle everybody's calls as rapidly as possible.

3. You Will Buy Only If . . .

In a way, this is the opposite of #2—a challenge to the reader's ego and pride. For example:

> . . . of course it takes a very special individual to fully appreciate the value of authentic Cromwell Crystal. Even though we've been very selective in choosing the people to receive this invitation, we also realize that only about 5 out of every 100 will respond.

4. You Can Buy Only If . . .

I've had many clients who market high-priced home-study courses, seminars, and tele-coaching programs on business, marketing, investing, and self-improvement, priced from $1,000.00 to $15,000.00 and more. Many use an "application process," to make people qualify to buy. But few of them have gone to the extremes one did. At various times, he required prospective purchasers to listen to 7 hours of introductory material and sign an official-looking affidavit attesting that they had done so before they were permitted to buy. Another client, a trade school, requires prospective students to furnish letters of reference.

A letter from a franchisor used the tactic this way:

> We are very particular about the people we select as business associates, so you're welcome to write or call for the free information kit, but don't get your hopes up just yet! Read everything thoroughly. Then, if you think you can qualify, you'll have to complete a detailed questionnaire, which will be reviewed by our Advisory Committee. Only if you are approved at that stage will you be invited to come to the Home Office for a personal interview.

5. Only Some Can Qualify . . .

This is a variation on #4. American Express has used this tactic for years in connection with its cards, particularly its Platinum Card. It appeals to the person's desire to be part of an elite group, for approval and recognition.

--- **Resource!** ---

I talk a great deal about "Takeaway Selling" in my book *No B.S. Sales Success.* Visit *www.nobsbooks.com.*

TECHNIQUE #2: Demonstrate ROI— Sell Money at a Discount

ROI is return on investment. In business-to-business sales letters, it's very important to talk about, promise, and if possible, demonstrate ROI. Even when marketing to consumers, it can be helpful to show that the proposed purchase actually costs nothing, thanks to the savings or profit it produces.

Demonstrating ROI puts you in the position of "selling money at a discount." Imagine having this job to do: stand in front of a crowd and offer as many $1,000.00 bills as anyone would like to buy—for $50.00 each. To start with, most people have never seen a $1,000.00 bill and would assume you were a counterfeiter, so you'd need experts there to attest to the authenticity of the product. Then you'd need to make it easy to buy, maybe by accepting Visa or MasterCard. And so on. But certainly if you did convince them that the bills were real and the offer was legitimate, you'd have no trouble unloading as much product as you wanted! Well, that's what you can do when you demonstrate ROI.

ROI can be presented in terms of dollars to be made. Here is some sample copy:

> Over 1,000 doctors reported specific increases in their incomes last year as a result of our course. Many reported net gains of $10,000.00 to $25,000.00. Once it's been repeated 1,000 times, it's no accident—it's a proven system you can use, too. Its cost? Just $199.00. So even a $1,000.00 income increase represents a 500% return on your investment!

ROI can also be presented in terms of dollars to be saved. For example, this copy:

> If you paid more than $300.00 in federal taxes last year, I guarantee this newsletter will be worth at least $150.00 to you—and it costs only $29.95! That's a 500% return on investment, guaranteed.

It sometimes pays to exaggerate our ROI promise, then bring the reader back down with copy like this:

> . . . and even if I'm only half right, you'll still pocket over $ . . .

This creates a feeling of reasonableness, conservatism, even objectivity—all reassuring to the reader.

TECHNIQUE #3: Ego Appeals

If everything bought in America in order to "keep up with the Joneses" were laid end to end, we'd probably have a durable-goods bridge reaching at least from here to Mars. Yes, ego is alive and well. When a product, a service, an association with a certain company, or any offer is convincingly portrayed as a status symbol, you've got the basis of a good sales letter.

There are many practical reasons for owning a fax machine. I rank it as one of the all-time best pieces of office equipment ever developed. But in talking with a marketer of such machines, very early in the game—when fax machines were still "new"—I realized that my ego, just as much as the convenience of the machine, was a motivating factor in my decision to purchase. The marketer and I discussed this, and came up with the following copy:

WHAT EXCUSE DO YOU MAKE
WHEN ASKED FOR YOUR FAX NUMBER—
AND YOU HAVEN'T GOT ONE?

Can you afford to appear "behind the times" to your clients, customers, vendors, and associates? Or is it important to you to be perceived as successful, savvy, in tune with the trends leading the American business scene?

Well, that "pitch" dates back to 1991. These days, every office and many homes have fax machines. But I hope you recognized the universal nature of that "pitch." It has been used to sell car phones when they were new, cell phones when they were new, Web sites when they were new. And whatever the next, new technology is that comes along, it too can and will be sold at some point based on ego appeal. Again, this is not limited to tech products. You'll see it used, for example, to sell the newest innovations in golf clubs, tennis rackets, automobiles, and on and on.

TECHNIQUE #4: Strong Guarantee

Some direct-marketing "authorities" have recently been pontificating about guarantees being out-of-date and ineffective with today's supposedly more sophisticated consumers. However, practical experience continues to prove that, first, a guarantee boosts response, and second, the better the guarantee, the better the response.

In fact, some research I've seen does indicate a heightened, harsher skepticism on the part of today's consumers. This is not just a consumer trend, but a societal one, largely supported by the repetitive failures of people we once looked up to. There's an endless parade of prominent people teaching the public to trust no one. In politics, you can go back to Nixon, to Oliver North, or more recently to Clinton's "I did not have sex with that woman." In religion, remember Jim and Tammy Faye Bakker, Jimmy Swaggart, and the Catholic Church's willingness to protect pedophile priests. As I write this edition, FDA-approved, widely prescribed, heavily advertised prescription drugs are being yanked out of the marketplace. The United Nations, supposed to be the world's arbiter on ethics, has been implicated in a gigantic international scandal. Every day it seems somebody's pouring another can of gasoline on the cynicism fire.

My conviction is that this calls for better, bolder, stronger guarantees—not abandonment of guarantees!

Here are the best ways to use a guarantee in your sales letters:

1. Basic Money-Back Guarantee

This is the simple, basic approach: If, for any reason, you are not fully satisfied with your purchase, return it for a full refund. I like to see this basic guarantee creatively embellished with livelier wording. You might say "delighted" or "thrilled" or even use fancier language, rather than "satisfied." You could opt for a folksier approach: ". . . return the widget for a full refund—no hassles, no hard feelings."

If it's unusual for a guarantee to be offered in your type of business, don't be bashful about saying so. For example: "Our guarantee is doubly important when you realize that no other widget maker offers one!"

2. Refund and Keep the Premium

You can strengthen your guarantee by linking it with a premium (free bonus gift). Example: "If you're not thrilled with your subscription, you may cancel, receive a full refund, and still keep the leather-bound appointment diary free, with our compliments! That's how absolutely certain we are that you will find tremendous value in every issue of . . ."

3. Redundancy

Another way to strengthen the presentation of your guarantee is to be deliberately redundant. Say the same thing twice or even three times! For example: "Receive a full 100% refund of every penny you paid."

4. Free Trial Offer

You can give your guarantee a different twist by presenting it as a free trial offer. Example: "You take no risk with our Free Trial Offer! If you're not happy with the Rocket-Z Weed Whacker, just return it anytime within 90 days for a full refund."

5. Make the Guarantee the Primary Focus of the Offer

You can sometimes increase the effectiveness of your entire sales letter by making the guarantee the featured item. The publisher of a financial newsletter achieved his greatest success when he started his sales letter this way:

Income tax savings guaranteed—or your money back! If, in the first three issues of my newsletter, you haven't found ways to decrease your taxes . . .

By the way, the use of a guarantee need not be limited to product offers. Many travel agents guarantee their customers the lowest available fares. Copier companies guarantee that their equipment will not exceed a specified amount of downtime. Restaurants guarantee lunch served in 15 minutes. With a little imagination and a genuine commitment to excellence, you can find a way to bring a guarantee into your marketing arsenal.

Now let me give you an advanced technique. This requires several things: first, brass balls; second, a real understanding of the prospects and how they'll behave; and third, a strong sales message you're certain will be of significant interest to the recipients of the sales letter. The daring strategy is to guarantee the letter. I actually use this strategy a lot, for myself and for clients. Often, we'll offer $10.00, $20.00, or $50.00 if the recipient reads the entire sales letter and feels his time has been wasted. An actual sample of this (Exhibit #13) comes from a very recent mailing I did for a seminar. In this case, I paid out less than $200.00 from mailing to nearly 4,000 prospects, but I brought in over $100,000.00 in profits. And we know from "split-testing" a number of times that the addition of "this letter is guaranteed" does increase readership and response.

In a somewhat similar fashion, I have a client in the financial services and asset protection business who sends out 100 of his sales letters on the first day of each month, targeting only owners or CEOs of corporations in his city who are known to have personal net worths exceeding $5 million. In his sales letter, he suggests that in just 19 minutes of conversation, he can reveal a dangerous "hole" in their financial fortresses or an opportunity to save on their income taxes that their current CPA, lawyer, or other advisors have not called to their attention. If he fails, he'll pay them $250.00 or donate $500.00 to the charity of their choice. With this courageous approach, he usually secures 10 to 15 appointments per 100 letters mailed (a 10 to 15 percent response) and then converts 2 to 3 of those into new clients, with an average first-year value per client of $10,000.00 or more.

Exhibit #13

> # This Free
> # Information
> # Package
> # Is Guaranteed
>
> How can something sent to you free be guaranteed? Here's my promise: if you read the attached, admittedly lengthy letter about your speaking business and listen to the enclosed audiocassettes and watch the enclosed video, and you honestly feel I've wasted your time, just jot me a note to that effect on the back of this certificate and I'll either pay you $25.00 or donate $50.00 to Habitat for Humanity, your choice.
>
> Since I'm sending out about 2,000 of these packages, that puts me on the hook for $100,000.00. That's okay, I can afford it. But I'm betting on your integrity as a professional colleague, and I'm betting on the fact that, even if you decide to say "no" to the offer extended to you in this informa-tion, at the very least you'll have to admit to picking up a valuable marketing idea or two you can use in your business, so this can't be a waste of time. Anyway, it's up to you. With my Guarantee, you can't lose by paying attention to this.
>
> Sincerely,
>
> [INSERT SIGNATURE]
>
> DAN S. KENNEDY
>
> NOTE: PLEASE (1) LISTEN TO THE "SPILL THE BEANS" AUDIOTAPE FIRST, THEN (2) WATCH THE VIDEO, THEN (3) READ THE LETTER, THEN (4) LISTEN TO THE "$25,000.00 A DAY" TAPE LAST. IT IS VERY IMPORTANT TO (AT LEAST) HEAR THE "SPILL THE BEANS TAPE" BEFORE READING THE LETTER.

TECHNIQUE #5: Be a Storyteller

If you want to take your sales letters to an advanced level, you'll have to become a great storyteller.

Storytelling is very powerful, because we all love a good story. We were conditioned as children to like them—"Read me a story! Tell me a story!" Fiction books far outnumber and outsell nonfiction books, and bestselling storytellers such as Stephen King, Tom Clancy, and John Grisham put one novel after another onto the bestseller lists.

I usually incorporate interesting stories in the sales letters I write and encourage others to do the same. I occasionally gather no more than ten people together for a three-day sales letter writing workshop, which costs $10,000.00 per person to attend, but I will let you in on a "secret" that I teach them, right here, free! Study good fiction and fiction writers, so you can write good stories and create good storylines for sales letters. At the workshop, I include story-writing exercises.

A good example is my Gold/VIP Member Darin Garman, to whom you were introduced in Section 1 of this book. Exhibit #14 is one of his national ads, and Exhibit #15 is the first page of one of his top-producing sales letters. As you'll see, they tell his personal life story, which is a dramatic, classic rags-to-riches tale.

———————————— **Resource!** ————————————

If you are a serious student of advanced copywriting, consider subscribing to my Look Over My Shoulder Program. Every month, I provide a collection of actual copywriting projects that I am working on for clients, from raw, first drafts to completed versions, with analysis. This is frankly an expensive program only for the very serious. Free information is at the publisher's Web site: *www.petetheprinter.com.* You can also obtain information about the Sales Letter Workshops at that same Web site. To learn storytelling skills, look into the many books about the craft of writing published by Writer's Digest Books. As a start, you can pick up a copy of *Writer's Digest* magazine at most newsstands.

Exhibit #14

"Former Iowa Prison Guard Shows Frustrated Investors How To Escape From Financial Prison And Truly Profit From America's Heartland!"

Darin Garman, CCIM
Consultant/Commercial
Real Estate Broker Of
Millionaires

In this FREE Report I reveal to investors with $75,000 or more to invest the easy to implement apartment and commercial property investment system, with a 10 year track record, that millionaire real estate investors are profiting from—here in the heartland of the U.S. With No Time Consuming Management Necessary—and how I discovered it years ago while working as a prison guard.

Even with a college degree, the best job that I could find after 4 years of college was working as a Prison Guard and not earning a very good living as a result. It was depressing and frustrating, at the time I wanted more for my wife and daughter, frankly, our family deserved better. So, out of frustration I searched for something better….and found it. What I accidentally discovered was investment real estate, specifically Iowa and Midwest properties. After my accidental discovery of the almost predictable profits and returns these investment properties had, I quit my job on the spot and started in the investment real estate business. That was 10 years ago. In this report I will share—

How For The Last 10 Years **Individual Investors from all over the United States have trusted me with over $151,344,433 Of Iowa And Midwest Real Estate Investments.**

That's correct. I have gone from being a prison guard to having assisted individual investors in building their wealth, predictably, hassle free and above all—profitably—Using Quality Real Estate Located In The Heartland Of The U.S.

For the last ten years I have been sharing **THE RIGHT WAY TO INVEST IN REAL ESTATE** with people as a broker and consultant. Today, I am the most sought after apartment and commercial property broker and consultant in the U.S. I have worked with many investors from beginners to millionaires to multi–millionaires, celebrities, etc. and have helped many become rich (or safely add to their wealth) using Iowa and Midwest apartment buildings and commercial property—located here in the heartland.

Now, I know you probably don't believe what I'm saying. Frankly, why should you? I'm as skeptical as anyone too. So, all I ask is that you give me 15 minutes of your time and I'll PROVE to you that I can help you build a safe and secure million dollar plus net worth (or safely add to it), using apartment and commercial property, right here in the heartland, with little risk and No management needed. **The nice thing is I found out accidentally (as a prison guard of all things) is its not that hard to do this, anyone can... If you let me share with you how, and this is important, HOW TO DO IT THE RIGHT WAY.** In just 15 minutes I'll show you how I discovered the secrets of successful commercial and investment property investors that no one really ever talks about. In fact, you will discover:

What This FREE Report Is NOT:

- NOT another get rich quick scheme
- NOT a "pitch" for some risky investment
- NOT a franchise offer
- NOT another "No Money Down" deal
- NOT an "Offering"

- Why Iowa and Midwest Apartments Are Better Than Any Other Investments, Even Single Family Homes, Stocks, Businesses, Etc.
- How To Easily Implement A Hassle Free Management System With Iowa Apartments That Frees You From Dealing With Or Worrying About Any Kind Of Tenant Problems and Complaints.
- Why Iowa and Midwest Apartment Properties Are The Best Kept "Auto Pilot" Wealth Secret Today And Why You Never Hear Anyone Talk About It.
- How To *Really* Break Through The Hype And Buy Iowa and Midwest Apartments For Large Monthly Cash Flow Profits With Very Little Risk—No Matter Where You Live.
- Discover The Inside "Tweak" You Can Use, Even Before You Take Over An Iowa Apartment or Commercial Property, That Can Easily and Immediately Raise The Value Over $10,000.
- How To Use The "Triple Hoop" Strategy, Only Used By Midwest Apartment Investors, To Make Sure You Walk Away From The Negotiating Table Knowing You Got The Best Deal.
- Find Out How You Can Legally Defer Capital Gains Taxes, Indefinitely If You Like, When You Invest In An Apartment And Commercial Property In Iowa...And Its Legal!

So, if you're tired and frustrated about getting your butt kicked in the market, your current income or the time its taking to reach your financial goals OR you just want to know how to invest in apartment/investment properties the smart way, the predictable way, with superior cash flow and superior returns while avoiding costly mistakes, this FREE NO OBLIGATION REPORT is for you. This report exposes the real strategies of successful millionaire apartment/commercial property owners and investors. **How To Get Your FREE Report:** Just call my FREE recorded message at 1-800-471-0856 and enter ID #3333. I only have 127 reports that can go out immediately so if interested delaying is not a good idea. You can call 24 Hrs. No one will talk to you.

Darin Garman, CCIM - Investment Property Specialist (#319-378-6748 Direct)

P.S. How To Get Your FREE Report: Just call my FREE recorded message at
1-800-471-0856 and enter ID #3333

Exhibit #15

Americas Top Commercial Real Estate Insider Finally Exposes The Real Secrets of The Hidden Real Estate Market No One Talks About...

"North America's Most Respected Commercial Real Estate Broker and Consultant Reveals The Secrets of Millionaire Commercial Real Estate Investors...Secrets That You've Never Heard Before"

Whether you're tired of the risk and slow returns of the stock market and other "traditional" investments or want enough cash flow coming in to quit your job in half the time...no where else will you find these closely guarded secrets to buildings wealth - until now.

Wednesday, 9:22 p.m.

Dear Friend:

My name is Darin Garman, CCIM – For the last 10 years I have been a Commercial Investment Real Estate Specialist acting as a consultant/agent for many wealthy investors. If you'd like to learn how these real estate investment secrets have broken the code on reaching your upper financial limits of massive cash flow and wealth building in a breathtakingly short time...and with a confident level of predictability...then this will be the most important message you will read in your life.

Here's my story: Ten years ago, thanks to Napoleon Hill, I decided to quit my job as a prison guard in Iowa (sounds glamorous, doesn't it?) and work in the world of commercial real estate. Actually, investment real estate. You know, apartment buildings, office buildings, shopping centers, etc.

Why am I saying that this all occurred thanks to Napoleon Hill?

Well, one day an empty liquor bottle was found in a garbage can right outside of my office in the prison. Of course I had no idea how an empty liquor bottle got inside the prison and into the garbage can outside of my office, but the Warden wanted some answers from me.

As I am sitting outside of the Wardens office, waiting to be questioned, I spot a worn out book on a book shelf. The title of the book was "**Think And Grow Rich**". Of course this is Napoleon Hill's classic.

Anyway, I started reading this book and it had a huge impact on my outlook in life. Such an impact that I quit my job there at the prison to pursue a burning desire. The desire to work in the world of commercial-investment real estate.. Why? Why would I do this?

Because I thought it would be profitable and also a lot of fun. I mean it had to beat the prison guard scene. So, being new and of course wet behind the ears, I jumped out of my prison guard job right into the world of investment real estate here in the heartland.

The Difference Was Unbelievable

I had my suspicions of how the world of commercial-investment real estate operated but you can imagine <u>my shock</u> at what kind of real estate outperformed all others AND how quickly this kind of property built the wealth of the investors that decided to invest in it. In other words, <u>I was shocked at how quickly these investors built their wealth over such a short period of time. And here's the interesting thing, you never hear people talk about this kind of real estate investment – I mean in Iowa??</u>

Write the First Draft

This chapter is short because its idea is a simple one. Put to work what you've learned so far!

Up until now, the steps of the system have put you through a great deal of preparatory work. Now you can start doing what you wanted to do in the first place: write!

You can now write a first draft. Don't edit as you go. Don't worry about length, grammar, or anything else—just write.

I usually wind up with a first draft that's two or even three times the length my letter ultimately winds up, but I prefer to get every possible persuasive idea onto the table and face the editing challenge later. I think this is, by far, the easiest of the many writing approaches I've seen copywriters use.

Drop your inhibitions, sharpen your pencil, and see what happens!

Rewrite for Strategy

You've written your first draft; it's probably too long. Now comes the rewrite stage.

This is a difficult process for a lot of writers, including me. We need to whittle away at the masterpiece we've created, to be certain it conveys the clearest possible message as concisely as possible. No, you needn't fear length. But you don't want sloppy length either. There's more to the rewriting step than just cutting length. In this chapter, we'll look at the "strategic" rewrites you can make to increase response to your letters.

Secrets of Successful Long Copywriting

"Who's going to read all that copy?" I can't tell you how many times I've been asked that question by a shocked, incredulous client staring at a sales letter that appeared to resemble a novel more closely than it did a note.

The answer is: those people most likely to respond.

Most research shows that the vast majority of readers never go beyond a quick glance at an advertisement, and the same is true of most sales letters. Even with excellent list selection, you'll still be sending your sales letters to a great many people who give them only a passing glance as they toss them into their wastebaskets. These people just are not interested in your product or service; they are not interested in *anything* at the moment except clearing their desks; they can't read; won't read; or for any number of other reasons are 100 percent resistant to your message. Worrying about whether this majority will read one page, half a page, or any other given quantity of copy is a foolish exercise—who cares? Trying to trick or manipulate these people into reading is extraordinarily difficult and of questionable value. Shortening your copy to a length everybody will read is counterproductive. Instead, we need to focus our energies on the relative minority of the letter recipients who will be interested in the message. In other words, write for the buyer, not the nonbuyer.

Real prospects are hungry for information—so says Ogilvy & Mather, one of the largest and most astutely run ad agencies in the world.

According to Ogilvy & Mather, research indicates that industrial ads with extensive text actually are read more thoroughly than are pieces with shorter copy. Readership drops precipitously for pieces that contain up to about 50 words; it drops much less between 50 and 500 words.

Early in my copywriting career, this kind of information inspired me to use long sales letters, usually 4 to as many as 16 pages. Rather than concern myself with the length of my letters, I chose to concentrate on telling seriously interested, qualified prospects everything they might possibly need to know to respond positively. If that required 16 pages, then 16 pages it was!

I have followed this principle for more than 20 years and am unwaveringly convinced of its validity. In some cases, we have started a campaign with a one- or two-page letter and gotten encouraging results; added a page or two and gotten better results; then added another page or two and gotten even better results!

Strategic Rewriting

Following are some guidelines that have proven successful for developing your sales letter at this stage.

Write and Rewrite Without Restraint

Have you ever wondered how there's just enough news each day to fit perfectly on the front page of the newspaper? Obviously, there isn't; articles are continued on subsequent pages, and some stories receive coverage for consecutive days, even weeks. Still, many reporters do write under editor-imposed length limits. So, to some degree, all the news that fits—be it 15 inches of needed column text or no more than 300 words—gets printed.

This is no way to sell. If you were a sales manager, would you send your representatives out into the field with the instruction, "Whatever you do, don't say more than 300 words"? I don't think so. Let's remember that a sales letter is a sales presentation in print.

It bears repeating: Do not write to fit a predetermined format or number of pages. Write to tell your story successfully.

Frustrate the English Teachers

My sales letters make lots of English teachers unhappy. They cringe and moan and groan. I've even occasionally received "critiques" from these dedicated grammarians. There's good reason for this: successful sales letters read much more like the way we talk than the way we're supposed to write. They use conversational English and popular slang. They often employ choppy sentences frowned on by style books: "It's a fact. It's guaranteed. It's proven. Under the intense heat and burning sun of the Salt Flats."

Schoolbook grammar is irrelevant in the sales letter. Instead, use every weapon in your arsenal—odd punctuation and phrasing, non-sentences, one-word exclamations, buzzwords—to push and prod and pull the reader along, and to create momentum and excitement.

Have you ever been around a young kid, maybe 10 or 12 years old, very excitedly telling you about some toy he or she wants, some place the kid wants to go, or something he or she wants to do? Excited kids talk so fast they stumble and stutter, rushing on without taking a breath. They never complete a sentence. And this enthusiasm is infectious. Inject that kind of action into your sales letter and you'll have a winner. Oh, and by the way—when you go to the bank to deposit all the profits your sales letter produced, nobody will ask whether you dangled a participle or split an infinitive while you were making the money.

Increase Readership with the Double Readership Path

We can divide our recipients into two personality extremes: the impulsive and the analytical. While most sales letters appeal to one extreme at the expense of the other due to the personality of the writer, we can appeal to both extremes in the same letter. *Analytical* prospects are logical, methodical people. If they are going to buy a new car, for example, they'll make a research project out of it. The *impulsive* prospect, on the other hand, buys a new car because it's red! It's obvious that these people should be addressed differently.

The impulsive ones will rarely read long copy, and, if they do, they'll read it only after heightening their interest by first somehow skimming the letter. For them, you need to "telegraph" your offer and its benefits. They want to skim and get the gist of your offer very quickly. These are impatient people, for whom you need to create an impulsive readership path through your letter that consists of big, bold headlines and subheads; photos with captions; and boxed, circled, or highlighted short paragraphs. While reading just those things, while running along that path, your impulsive reader needs to get enough information to respond.

Frequently, after skimming, the impulsive prospect will slow down and read and consider the entire long sales letter. This is our goal.

For the analytical prospect, we can provide a more complete readership path. The impulsive path becomes just the signposts along the analytical path. The analytical prospects will read long copy—in fact, they almost require it! They want lots of facts, figures, statistics, charts, graphs, and hard information, wanting to feel that they are making an informed, considered decision.

In the example that follows (Exhibits #16 and #17), we've highlighted the impulsive path, so you can see how it hops through the letter. The analytical path follows this same order, but every word is read along the way.

Exhibit #16

THE SILVER INVESTMENT OF THE DECADE

These 100 pesos silver dollars are priced to sell at only $8.75 each in quantity . . . way below normal rates. When you compare the price, choice, brilliant condition, and profit potential to any, and we do mean any, other silver coin investments, you will find this to be the best silver deal ever.

THE ULTIMATE IN PRIVACY

100 pesos silver dollars are private . . . completely exempt from the IRS reporting required of coin dealers on form 1099-B. Many investors demand complete privacy to buy and sell without a lot of government snooping . . . these coins are 100% fully exempt.

MAKE 1000% BY 1992?

Experts in many of the financial journals, people like Bill Kennedy of Western Monetary, the Aden Sisters, Howard Ruff, and others predict silver could blow the lid off and hit $25–$50 or even $100 per ounce by 1992 . . . if the financial fiasco boiling in Washington erupts. When this comes about, the 100 pesos could melt for as much as $70 per coin.

Exhibit #17

RICH IN SILVER CONTENT

These giant coins weigh nearly one ounce and are 72% pure in silver quality. The fact is, they offer 6 times as much silver for your money as BU Morgan silver dollars. And as silver prices climb in coming years, the value of these heavy coins should skyrocket. It's like having risk insurance on your silver investment. As incredible as it may seem, you can now own 6 of these big Mexican cartwheels in brilliant uncirculated condition for the price of just one common date U.S. Morgan dollar.

TIMING IS URGENT

The AMARK secret is beginning to leak out now . . . thus eliminating your chance of big profits. Don't wait until the cat's out of the bag! Buy now!! Next week or next month could be a red letter profit day for many astute silver investors who heed our advice today.

A CLASSIC FROM SILVER-RICH OLD MEXICO

As a big fan of the entire category of Mexican silver dollar size coins, I was excited when these factors came together . . . just at the right time . . . creating an unparalleled time to buy. Due to the latest Mexican financial crisis, you can buy coins at a small fraction above their actual intrinsic value—a remarkable paradox to say the least. And because this is the last of the great big high-silver content pesos coins in Mexican history . . . it's a classic!

Say It Again, Sam. And Again. And Again.

Can you fill in these blanks?

> *Pepsi-Cola hits (blank) (blank);*
> *(blank) (blank) (blank) —*
> *that's a lot!*

> *Lucky Strike means (blank) (blank).*

> *Double your (blank),*
> *Double your (blank),*
> *With (blank), (blank), (blank) gum.*

> *At Burger King, you can (blank) (blank) (blank) (blank).*

> *It's (blank) time.*

These are very old advertising slogans that many people can still recall perfectly and instantly. Why? Did people make a special point of memorizing those slogans? Of course not! They learned and memorized this information automatically, as a result of massive repetition. In fact, that's one of only two ways that we accept new ideas and information as valid—through repetition. The other way is shock.

Let me give you an example: selling home security systems. A great many people invest in such systems immediately after their homes have been broken into. They accept the idea of the worth and importance of such a product thanks to the shock of having their home invaded, burglarized, maybe even vandalized. The only other way they will come to accept this idea and invest in a system is by being repetitively exposed to persuasive information.

In public speaking, there is a time-honored axiom: tell 'em what you're going to tell 'em; tell 'em; tell 'em; then tell 'em what you've told 'em. I've expanded it to: tell 'em what you're going to tell em; tell 'em; tell 'em again, a little differently; tell 'em again, a little more differently; then tell 'em what you've told 'em. In fact, I try to tell 'em seven times. I do this in my speeches and seminars. I do it in my sales letters, too. I call it internal repetition.

In the same sales letter, you can convey your basic sales message and promise:

1. In a straightforward statement
2. In an example
3. In a story, sometimes called a "slice of life"
4. In testimonials
5. In a quote from a customer, expert, or other spokesperson
6. In a numbered summary

A "manufactured example" that uses all these methods appears as Exhibit #18.

Exhibit #18

4 ACES CARPET CLEANING SPECIALISTS
123 Success Street
Cleansville, USA 123456

Dear Briarwood Area Homeowner,

You've probably lived in your home for three, four, maybe even five years, and in that time a lot of "traffic" has taken its toll on your carpets.

We guarantee to make your carpeting look like new, or there's no charge for our services!

Here's how it works: We'll come to your home, by appointment. First, we'll test the "worst spot." If you judge that job successful, we'll do that whole room. You continue to be the judge, room by room. You pay only for what you approve. And, during the next 21 days, you get one room FREE for every three cleaned. For example, a typical Briarwood home with an # × # carpeted living room, a # × # carpeted family room, and two # × # carpeted bedrooms will get one bedroom's carpeting CLEANED FREE!

Like new again—no matter what!

We were recently called to one home where, while the parents were away, the teenagers' "little party" had gotten out of control: beer stains, soda pop stains, ground-in mud and grime, and a few things we never definitely identified! Here's what that homeowner, Mrs. Trusting Parent on Elm Street, said after our visit:

"When I saw the living room carpet after the kids' party, I just knew we'd have to buy all new carpeting. I tried some carpet cleaner liquid I bought at the store, and it just made it worse. But, in just one hour, the guys from 4 Aces had it perfectly clean! I'm still amazed every time I look at it!"

Act now—call us today at 239-ACES and . . .

1. Schedule a FREE Consultation and Cost Quotation
2. We'll clean your carpets room by room
3. You judge our job as we go
4. You pay only for the work you approve
5. You get one room FREE for every three charged
6. Your satisfaction is guaranteed

Hank, Bill, Tom, & Larry,
"The 4 Aces"

Move Your Reader Along with a Yes Sequence

Recently a hypnotherapist reminded me of a basic principle of persuasion: building a "yes momentum." You develop receptivity to your offer by giving your readers a sequence of "knowns" they can easily agree with and questions they can easily say "yes" to. This gets them in the habit of agreeing with you.

You might incorporate this idea in a sales letter by starting or ending each paragraph with a question, or using questions as subheads. Asking questions involves the reader.

Tease the Reader at the End of Each Page

First, a format tip: never end a page with a completed sentence. This gives your reader permission to stop reading right there. Instead, always end each page in the middle of a sentence, preferably right in the middle of an interesting or exciting phrase. This spurs the reader on to the next page where, once started, he or she is likely to finish.

In addition, you may want to add teaser copy at the bottom of each page. This is an opportunity to use a graphic device, by the way, such as simulated handwriting or yellow fake highlight. A blurb of teaser copy is something like this:

The Author's 7 secrets for beating the stock market,

revealed on the next page!

How we saved $38,000.00 in repairs the first year—

even though we were skeptics! See the next page!

Now, from these examples, did you pick up on the secret to creating good teaser copy? A teaser blurb is essentially another headline. In fact, it is a headline for the next page! So you use the principles for creating successful headlines to create your teaser blurbs, too.

Rewrite for Style

Beyond the mechanics, the teaser lines, and the readership paths lies the question of your letter's general strength of delivery. In this chapter we'll look at some of the most effective ways to make your letter stand out as "a good read."

Increase Readership by Improving Readability

What is readability? The computer industry uses the term "user friendly." I think they apply this rather loosely, but it is supposed to mean that the computer is easy to use, uses everyday language, and does not require you to be a rocket scientist to operate it. I think sales letters should be reader friendly. That means the letter appears easy to read, is easy on the eye, uses everyday language, and doesn't require you to be a Harvard grad or a determined masochist to get through it.

A good copywriter creates this reader friendliness with a number of devices that nurse the reader along—that push, prod, pull, entice, and motivate. These devices include short, punchy sentences and even shorter non-sentences. You should also stick mostly to short paragraphs (ideally, those only three or four sentences long).

Use the First Paragraph as an Extended Headline

Think of it this way: In the first paragraph, you sell the recipient on reading your letter; then in the rest of the letter, you sell your proposition. Here's an example of a poorly used first (and second) paragraph in an otherwise reasonably good sales letter—and a repaired version.

**Emergency Memo for
Preferred Clients**

I would have taken the time to write you a personalized letter, but in this instance I believe that getting the information into your hands pronto is more important. Even our Marketing Department requested I bypass them and go directly to our most concerned silver investors.

You've probably been watching the silver market lately, and as you may have guessed, market indicators show that silver is getting ready to make a surge. But many of our silver buyers have been afraid to buy bullion due to possible IRS reporting, and have asked for our recommendation as the next best thing to buy for investors who value their privacy.

Here's my rewrite:

**Emergency Memo for Preferred Clients Direct
From Brent Lee, Research Department**

*Market indicators show that silver is getting ready to make a surge! But many of our silver buyers have been afraid to buy bullion, due to possible IRS reporting, and have asked us for help. Now we have the answer—just what the doctor ordered for savvy silver investors who value their privacy—fully explained in this important letter!

*Letter excerpt used courtesy of Chattanooga Coin Co., Box 80158, Chattanooga TN 37411.

Be Entertaining

No, don't be funny. Outright humor rarely works in sales letters and is too difficult for anyone but an experienced pro to carry off. There are safer, surer paths to follow. On the other hand, you may not want to be funeral-serious throughout your letter, either. In fact, there's no such thing as too much interesting copy. The problem's not with the length. The problem is being boring.

Here's the beginning of a letter I sent to a group of people who travel incessantly (as I do). As you'll see, it is lighthearted; not comical, but not dead serious.

> Last night, I left a Wake-Up-And-What-City-Am-I-In-And-What-Day-Is-This call at my hotel. Maybe I'm traveling just a little too much! How about you? Just recently, I've discovered a way to earn lots of money in our business without squeezing into the big silver tube and heading off for distant lands. If you'll give me 15 minutes of your time to read this letter thoroughly, I'll share every profitable detail with you right now!

A dead serious version of the same copy might look like this:

> Tired of traveling? There is a way to earn lots of money in your business without travel. Read this letter and learn more about it.

Which is more fun to read?

Appeal to the Senses

Although we consciously think mostly in terms of sight, our more powerful subconscious system takes in input from all five senses all the time.

I believe that the reader's "whole mind" can best be stimulated by playing on as many of the five senses as possible.

Consider, for instance, the idea of selling a good, fast computer by describing the unpleasant experience of being the last person left working late, alone, in a big, dark, cold office. Remember, your sales letter copy needs to make the reader visualize pictures and feel experiences.

Use Big Impact Words and Phrases

Consider this incredible example of words on paper that absolutely commands attention and evokes emotion:

> There was a desert wind blowing that night. It was one of those hot dry Santa Anas that come down through the mountain passes and curl your hair and make your nerves jump and your skin itch. On nights like that every booze party ends in a fight. Meek little wives feel the edge of the carving knife and study their husbands' necks. Anything can happen.

That's from the late, great mystery novelist Raymond Chandler. As a frustrated novelist myself, I love passages like that—and I have found them useful in sales letters. And if you find writing whole blocks of copy like that too tough, at least plug in "charged" phrases here and there.

Here are a few such phrases I've found or thought up and used in various sales letters:

- Serious as cancer
- Stronger 'n onions!
- Savage wind
- So overcome with frustration, he leans against the closed door of his office and silently screams
- Crawl across broken glass on your naked knees to . . .
- So powerful (so good; so tasty; so _____) it should be illegal

Here's an example of a subhead from a recent sales letter I wrote for our businesses:

Why You Should Put On a Ski Mask,
Lower Yourself From the Ceiling On a Wire
Like Tom Cruise In "Mission Impossible,"
To Steal Bill's Blueprint

This is merely a variation on "why you should crawl across broken glass on your naked knees to . . ." It is the same idea, delivered in the same way, creating a vivid mental picture.

I've built up a fairly large card file of such phrases, culled from advertising, television, novels, all sorts of sources. I suggest that you do the same. These kinds of phrases add bursts of color to your copy.

Resource!

Reference books that copywriters use to find and create colorful, descriptive phrases:

Words That Sell by Richard Bayan (Contemporary)

More Words That Sell by Richard Bayan (Contemporary)

Roget's Superthesaurus by Marc McCutcheon (Writer's Digest Books)

Roget's Descriptive Word Finder by Barbara Ann Kipfer (Writer's Digest Books)

Also, for great examples of vivid, descriptive language, enroll in the free 12-week Ultimate Sales Letter e-mail course at *www.Ultimate-Sales-Letter.com*.

Make Your Letter Reflect Your Own Personal Style

I admit here that I don't know how to tell you how to do this. I only know that some letters have personality and others don't. Some letters give you the feeling that you're hearing from a real human being, a unique individual; others don't.

The best sales letter writers I know have their own unique styles. I can usually tell their work in my own incoming mail by this style, and I'm right about 90 percent of the time.

Let your own personality come into your letters. Sell in print as you would in person.

Answer Questions and Objections

Unanswered questions and unresolved concerns sabotage sales letters! By carefully countering every possible question and objection, you put the ultimate sales presentation on paper.

The Reasons Why Not

In person-to-person selling, there is a step typically referred to as "overcoming objections." At some point, the prospect is going to raise one or (more likely) several objections, and it is up to the salesperson to counter or neutralize those objections effectively. Some salespeople welcome this exercise because they believe it indicates real interest on the prospect's part. Others fear and loathe this part of selling. But whatever the individual salesperson's past experience and attitude toward customer objections, they will come up in almost every sale, and they must be dealt with.

Live salespeople have several big advantages over the sales letter writer in facing objections. First, they have the luxury of responding only to those objections raised by the individual customer. Second, they get immediate feedback to determine whether they need to tell more. Third, they can "box in" the customer to turn the objection-answering process into a sure sale. There is, for example, a selling tactic known as "draining the objections," in which salespeople list the objections on a pad before answering any. They keep asking "Anything else?" until the customer runs dry of objections. Then they ask, "If we can take care of all these concerns to your satisfaction—and I'm not sure that we can—but if we can, you will then want to go ahead with the XYZ tonight, right?" When the customer says "yes" to that, he or she is boxed in. There's no way I've found to duplicate that process in print.

Our sales letter does not have the luxury of responding only to the objections each recipient thinks of. The letter has to respond to every possible objection. Our letter does not get any feedback that would make it clear when "enough is enough," so it must do more than enough.

I've sat in meetings with clients and advertising pros and had them argue vehemently against raising any objections in a sales letter. Why put negative thoughts in a reader's mind? While I avoid overestimating a customer's intelligence, I try never to underestimate skepticism! Those marketers who think they can "hide" the objectionable issues are grossly underestimating the skepticism of customers. If customers are going to think of anything, they are going to think of all the reasons not to buy.

As it happens, I've had great success with a copywriting formula that airs the likely objections for the customer, and then answers them. The start of that copy block reads something like this:

> As attractive as this product/service/offer is, our marketing experts tell us that only about X% of the people receiving it will respond. Although that's okay with us from a business standpoint, it still bothers me personally. You see, I know how much the owners/users of our product/service/offer benefit from it. I read their letters; I talk to them on the phone; I see them personally when they visit us; and hundreds/thousands/millions each year tell me that "(strong, brief customer quote)." Because of this, I just hate the thought of someone not getting our product/service/offer because of some error or omission in our explanation. That's why I held a special brainstorming

session with a group of our people just to try to figure out why you might say "no" to our free trial offer. After several hours, our group could think of only three possible reasons.

Here they are:

After a setup like that, I would list each reason for not buying and then respond to it.

Another, more commonly used (and, I think, wimpier, though still effective) version of this formula is to include a page of "Frequently Asked Questions and Answers" with the sales letter. The anticipated objections are phrased as questions and answered.

In either case, the answers to most objections or questions should include most of these items—and in most instances, all of them:

1. A direct answer
2. A verifying testimonial comment, case history, or story
3. A restatement of or reference to the guarantee/free trial offer

Spark Immediate Action

When you play the sales letter game, you go up against some pretty difficult mathematics: X percent of your letters never get delivered to the intended recipients, Y percent of the letters are discarded unopened, and Z percent reach people who, for one reason or another, cannot or will not respond, no matter how good the offer is. But quite probably, the biggest group of nonrespondents are those who get the letter, look at the letter, read the letter, and intend to respond to the letter—but set it aside to do "later." All too often, "later" never happens.

The Mañana Antidote: How to Get Immediate Response

In most cases, most of the response to a sales letter will come in almost immediately. Yes, there will be a "trickle effect," and you will get some response weeks or even months after mailing the letter—from people who set the letter aside, buried it under a pile of papers, waited until they could afford to respond, or had any number of other reasons to procrastinate. This trickle, though, is virtually insignificant in terms of the profitability of a letter campaign. You go to the bank with the immediate response. For this reason, you must give careful thought to every possible way you can increase the urge to respond immediately.

One of my mentors in copywriting used to tell me: "Imagine your letter being read by a guy in an apartment in Cleveland, in the midst of a ferocious winter storm, with gusting winds and snow outside at thigh height. You've got to get him so excited that he'll get out of the chair in front of the fireplace, bundle up, slog through the snow, go out to his cold car, and drive down to the post office to get a money order and a stamp to send his order in—rather than take the risk of waiting until tomorrow."

Of course, the job is rarely that tough, because customers can respond to most sales letters by phone, calling toll-free numbers and paying by credit card. Still, the idea is the same. Responding is sometimes inconvenient. Usually, your letter's recipient is busy and preoccupied with other matters. There is tremendous temptation to stop at a "conditional yes"—setting the letter aside with the intention of responding "tomorrow."

Your letter's job is to get the reader to respond right now.

Here are the seven most powerful ways I know of to stimulate immediate response.

1. Limited Availability

If you are honestly making an offer in which either the primary product or the premium or a discount or rebate is limited by availability, you can try to convince the recipient that "the race is on!"

2. Premiums

It is rare for the basic offer to be strong enough in and of itself to inspire immediate response from a satisfactory number of people. Because of this, I am a strong advocate of using premiums, and usually prefer a premium over a discount or rebate. It has often been my experience that the right premium offer can make as much as a 50 percent positive difference in response to a sales letter.

An example of both of these strategies combined in a single letter comes from Bob Stupak, the creator of the Vegas World Hotel (now the Stratosphere) in Las Vegas—in my opinion, the shrewdest marketer that entire city has ever seen.

For years, Vegas World sold a package including lodging, drinks, entertainment, and a gambling bankroll for a set price through print ads, direct mail, and television. If you bought the package and went, as soon as you returned home you received an invitation to buy that same package again and use it in the future. Many people became repeat purchasers of these packages and came to realize that they could get one just about whenever they wanted it, so the usual urgency-building techniques—like an ordering deadline—no longer worked on those people. They became immune to those offers. As a result, Bob Stupak developed the letter that is shown as Exhibit #19A (on page 123). A lengthy paragraph, which is not included here, describes a Hawaiian package. Then, the letter continues as shown in Exhibit #19B (on page 123).

The next paragraphs, which are not shown in the Exhibits, describe the Vegas World package, making the important point that it is the same package at the same price as always.

There are several enclosures with this letter that reinforce the core offer and the premium. Does it work? Well, it got me! The morning it arrived in my mail at the office, I was busier than the proverbial one-armed paper hanger and certainly had no intention of buying another Vegas World package that day—but I stopped what I was doing, read the letter, got on the phone, and ordered immediately. Why?

1. I knew and trusted the company (Vegas World).
2. I liked the product (the Vegas World package).
3. I believed the urgency-building story (only 1,000 Hawaiian vacations available).
4. I found the premium exciting and desirable.

Duplicate those four factors in a sales letter, and you'll have a winner, too. In fact, I urge you to write those four factors down on a card or sheet of paper and keep it visible, wherever you work and will write your sales letters. If you engineer a selling environment in which these four factors exist and can be carried over to your sales letter, you are virtually guaranteed success.

Here's a business-to-business sales letter example utilizing the same strategy, from a publisher of educational videotapes for use in sales training:

FREE TV AND VCR—BUT YOU MUST CALL NOW!

We've made a special purchase, direct from a major Japanese manufacturer, of just 250 19-inch color TV monitors with built-in VCRs. If purchased in a store, this model might cost you $499.00 to as much as $899.00. But you can get one free, as a gift, with your purchase of any one of our three new Video Training Systems described in the enclosed brochure. You already know the fantastic quality and effectiveness of our systems—you own at least one of them already. Now you can get one of our newest systems—plus a free TV/VCR. But you must act immediately. We have only 250 of these TV/VCRs and cannot obtain any more.

Exhibit #19A and B

From the Desk of Bob Stupak

Dear Mr. and Mrs. Kennedy:

I am writing to just a fraction of my previous guests for this first-time offer. This is a test and may never be repeated again.

SIX DAY, FIVE NIGHT HAWAIIAN VACATION

I have entered into a contract with Holiday Travel of America, one of the nation's largest fully bonded wholesale travel agencies, and have paid in advance for over 1,000 Hawaiian vacation packages to present as gifts to my returning previous guests.

When you again accept your fabulous Vegas World invitation with us, we will immediately send you your documents for a wonderful Hawaiian vacation for two.

But please remember, this is a test and is being offered to only a fraction of our previous guests and may never be offered again. This offer is available only until Thursday, November 1st, or until our allotted number of Hawaiian vacations is gone, whichever comes first, so I urge you to act quickly.

3. Deadlines

The deadline is the most basic and common urgency-builder. It can stand alone or be used in combination with any of the other strategies.

If your mailings are small, you'll give extra impact to the deadline date by having it handwritten or rubber-stamped on your letter. If quantity prohibits that, you might work with your artist and printer to simulate a handwritten or rubber-stamped appearance.

An insurance agent friend of mine was in the habit of mailing out 100 letters each week to cold prospects compiled from his local street directory, offering a free road atlas just for letting him quote prices on auto insurance. Typically, he'd get one, two, or three responses from each hundred—which, incidentally, is pretty darned good in such a situation. At my suggestion, he changed the letter to offer the free road atlas only if the recipient responded by a certain date; the date was rubber-stamped in red ink on the letter. His response went from 1 to 3 percent to 5 to 8 percent.

4. Multiple Premiums

I've often found that if one is good, two is better! When a premium offer proves successful, it's usually smart to then test a double-premium offer.

A company selling cleaning, deodorizing, and safety chemicals via sales letters experienced considerable success when it added the offer of a free locking storage cabinet with a certain-size order received within 15 days. When I saw the dramatic increase in response that the addition of this premium caused, I suggested testing a double premium. The company then offered one cabinet with an $X order or two cabinets with a larger $Y order. While the overall response percentage remained virtually the same, the average order size increased by nearly 30 percent!

5. Discounts for Fast Response; Penalties for Slow Response

This strategy is used a lot in the seminar business. Take a look at the next few seminar brochures that cross your desk and you'll undoubtedly see pricing schedules that look like this:

ENROLL BY JANUARY 15: $149.00 per person

ENROLL AFTER JANUARY 15 BUT BEFORE FEBRUARY 20: $199.00 per person

AT THE DOOR (if available): $229.00 per person

This same strategy could be applied to advance-order offers tied to new, soon-to-be-released products; any kind of event tickets or passes; subscriptions or subscription renewals; and other offers.

6. Sweepstakes and Contests

Who hasn't received an envelope with Ed McMahon's smiling face on the outside? ("You may be our next millionaire winner!") Sweepstakes and contests have entry deadlines, so they spark immediate response. They are used not only by subscription agencies such as American Family Publishers and Publishers Clearing House, but also by car companies, industrial manufacturers, service businesses, and others. They are admittedly expensive but seem to repay their investments many times over in increased response.

7. Ease of Responding

Essentially, the easier it is for the person to respond, the better. Offering a toll-free number always boosts response tremendously, and depending on the nature of your business, the letter recipients, and economics, having that number manned 24 hours a day, 7 days a week, and/or enclosing preaddressed response cards or envelopes may prove beneficial.

Surprisingly, including postage-paid response devices rarely enhances response enough to justify the added expense. If you are going to do this, you should test it both ways—you may discover that the cost is unwarranted.

You should also consider inviting response by fax, with a form included for that purpose; via your Web site, by entering information there and/or downloading information; and even via e-mail.

The Creative P.S.

Every sales letter needs a P.S.—do not consider your efforts complete until you have composed one. The P.S. can make or break your letter!

Use the P.S. to Stimulate Readership

Yes, many people skip to the end of the letter first. Some want to look at the signature, to try to identify who is writing to them. Others are just perverse—they also read the end of a mystery novel before buying it, and they eat their dessert first. Their perversity is your opportunity! By properly summarizing the offer or promise in your P.S., you can inspire the recipient to dig in and read the entire letter, or simply add an extra incentive to respond.

P.S.: Even if your reader has read the text in the "proper" sequence, the P.S. serves as a high-impact "second headline" you can ill afford to ignore!

Check the Checklists

You have now written several drafts, and you've made heaven only knows how many changes and corrections in the surviving draft. If you wind up working the way I do, your draft will look like the homework you used to claim your dog ate.

For more than 20 years, I traveled constantly, some years well over 150,000 air miles. These days, most clients come to me, but still, every time I board an airplane, I am glad that pilots operate with checklists. After all, how many times have you simply forgotten to do something you know you should do? (Yesterday, I got out of my car without putting it into "Park" or turning off the engine; the car lurched against the parking block and sat there groaning, grumbling under its breath about its idiot owner. Obviously, I'm a big believer in checklists.) This step is the way to be certain you incorporate as many successful strategies, formulas, and techniques as possible into your sales letter. It is sort of a midcourse correction. You are about halfway through the entire system—the process of writing your sales letter—and this is a good time to make a number of little adjustments.

Use Graphic Enhancement

Now it's time to do a draft of your letter on your PC and start to jazz it up with graphic devices. This is a very important step. It is something that, as a freelance copywriter, I've specialized in, taking care to control the appearance of the piece, not just the words. In this chapter, you will find many ways to "supercharge" a sales letter. This is one of several chapters in this book that are much more comprehensive compared to prior editions. In the 15 years that have elapsed since I wrote the first edition, my appreciation for the importance of this step has grown immensely.

Give Your Letter an Easy-to-Read Appearance

The sales letter writer should collaborate closely with the typesetter or typist, layout artist, and printer to use as many "graphic devices" as possible to make the long copy look (perhaps deceptively) easy to read.

The truth of the matter is that today's consumer is lazier than ever. Consider the popularity of the TV remote control, the microwave, the cell phone, passive exercise machines. Look around: we don't do things, we have things done for us. We don't want it fast—we want it now!

These are the graphic devices I use most often to make a long sales letter look like an easier and faster read:

1. Bullets ■ ■ ■
2. Numbering: 1, 2, 3, and so on
3. <u>Underlining</u>
4. **Boldfacing**
5. *Varied **type***
6. *Simulated handwriting*—in the margins, in the P.S.
7. Boxes
8. Lines made of asterisks ***************
9. Yellow overprint (an option in your word processing program allows your printer to use yellow ink to simulate sloppy markings made with a yellow highlighter pen)
10. Screens (washes of a light dot pattern over a paragraph or two; you can use a gray screen if printing in black, or a pastel screen from your primary accent color, such as pink from red)
11. Photographs with type running around them
12. **Subheads** . . . lots and lots of subheads!

Contrary to what many people in the advertising business believe, these choices about graphic devices should not be left up to the typesetters and artists. The person who writes the copy must have direct involvement in suggesting, considering, and deciding on the use of these devices. The main purpose of these graphic enhancements is not to improve the aesthetic appearance of the letter; it is to add "voice inflection" to the copy—and the copywriter is best qualified to choose what to emphasize and how to emphasize it.

One of the most effective enhancements to boost readership is personalization. Personalized mailings were once difficult to do and looked clumsy, but today's technology allows for personalization of headlines, body copy, enclosures, even pre-filled-out, personalized order forms.

One of my favorite recent examples was done with a mailing I developed for Rory Fatt at Restaurant Marketing Systems. In connection with this seminar, a new Chrysler Crossfire convertible was being given away. Each recipient of the mailing saw his or her first name on the oversized license plate on the photograph of the car.

You'll find value in building up an "idea file" from the mail you receive, so you can show other project participants exactly what you want.

———————————— **Resource!** ————————————

The leading printing and mailing company expert in personalized mailings is Think Ink. You can get information by faxing a request to 714-374-7071.

The Illustrated Sales Letter

One of the most exciting ways to spice up a sales letter is illustrating it throughout with photographs, drawings, charts, graphs, and testimonials, all presented in a graphically interesting way.

My Platinum Member Ted Thomas is an absolute master of this art. Several of his illustrated sales letters, which have produced well over $500,000.00 for him, are shown here. Exhibit #20 (page 133) is the first page/front cover of an 8-page sales letter for one of the seminars for investors that he presents every year. Exhibit #21 (page 134) is page 5 of that same piece, headlined "My Husband Was Stunned." Look at all the different typestyles and sizes, the little cartoon, checkmarks, magnifying glass, starburst, and photo, all on this page. Ordinary graphic artists in typical ad agencies would scream bloody murder about this layout—but they're wrong, and Ted is right. Split tests between a "pretty," neat, organized, perfect piece and an "ugly," jumbled piece prove it. Exhibit #22 (page 135) is, in real life, a two-sided flyer on garish pink paper, with a neon green sticky note in its center. I've shown you the side with the sticky note here. This, too, goes in the same mailing, which contains more than 20 pages in all.

———— Resource! ————

You might wonder how this works in a more ordinary business. Here's a letter I got from Gold/VIP Member Scott Tucker, a mortgage broker (and marketing coach to mortgage brokers):

"Here is the very first sales letter I ever wrote, after reading your *Ultimate Sales Letter* book and going through your Copywriting Seminar In A Box. It mailed as an eight-page booklet, black text on white paper, with the scrawled handwritten notes in blue ink. The whole mailing cost me $1.00 each, $5,000.00 for 5,000 pieces. It brought in $40,000.00 in fee income from funded loans in the first 30 days. That was welcome income as I had just gone out on my own after being fired from a job as a loan officer. I paid for the first mailing with my Discover Card! In total, it brought in over $75,000.00 in 60 days. So the ROI from my first sales letter was 15 times cost! I kept mailing it and after the first 4 months, my bank account was bulging. I celebrated by taking a 10 day vacation to France, Belgium, the Netherlands and Switzerland. I paid off my truck, bought a new laptop. The letter became the foundation of my business. It's allowed me to change the lives and be of help to thousands of Chicagoans you'll never meet—I've helped them avoid bankruptcies, un-do car repossessions, get their financial lives back on track. Now I'm helping hundreds of mortgage brokers do the same in their cities. All thanks to this odd, junked-up, illustrated sales letter. Thanks!"

Exhibit #20

Starting This Month, You Can LOCK-IN 16% Returns On Your Investment Dollars

Starting Right Now, You Can Get High Returns By Investing In Tax Certificates

27,168 Tax Lien Certificates Will Be Auctioned Starting At 8:30am On February 14 In Phoenix, Arizona

I'm Planning To Attend That Auction...

Before The Auction Begins...
I plan to check out and evaluate the properties — **In A Large Tour Bus** — You could ride along with me!

Then I plan to research all the nitty-gritty property details at the County Public Records. You could come with me and my staff of experts and learn the tricks of the trade.

If You Take Action Quickly... You can attend 3 days of Auction Workshop Classes and a Bonus 4th day going to the auction with us on the bus.

Take Action Before December 9th and you'll SAVE $500!

Ted Thomas   Created and copyrighted © 2004 by Ted Thomas™ and Jones & Trevor Marketing • 321-449-9940 • FAX 321-449-9938

Exhibit #21

My Husband Was "Stunned"

In Less Than Two Months, These "Little Known" Government Certificates Produced A 25% Return!

Redeemed $9,187.50

It all happened like this... Cheryl attended a short instruction course conducted by Ted Thomas in Phoenix, Arizona. After just a few days of instruction, Cheryl put the concept she learned to work. This "Hidden Market" is open to all North Americans to take advantage of. While vacationing in **Texas, Cheryl invested $7,390 in a Tax Certificate,** which was issued by Limestone County. Officially, there are over 3,000 government agencies just like Limestone County in the United States that sell Tax Lien Certificates or Tax Deed Certificates.

Profit: $1,797.36

Ted Thomas'™

The Tax Lien & Deed Info-Source

I'm Sure You Are Skeptical, I Felt The Same Way. *Then I Watched As These Techniques And Strategies Were "Tested" In A TED THOMAS Workshop In Front Of More Than 100 Eager Investors.*

Cheryl Hyland, Canada Holding Her "Profit" Checks

25% RETURN

Cheryl invested $7,390 on March 7 and on July 18, she received $9,187.50 in return. That's 4 months and 11 days to make $1,797.50, 25% return on a passive investment, which was guaranteed to pay her.

You Can't Make This Kind Of Money Anywhere!

Created and Copyrighted ©2004 by Ted Thomas™ and Jones & Trevor Marketing • 321-449-9940 • Fax 321-449-9938   **5**

Exhibit #22

Exhibits #23, #24, and #25 (pages 137, 138, and 139) are three pages chosen from the entire letter. As you'll see, there are photos, a comparison chart, and a lot of deliberately messy handwriting used to make this letter stand out and intrigue the reader.

Resource!

Scott has a national coaching group for mortgage brokers, and he invites them to contact him via *www.mortgagemarketinggenius.com* or by faxing 773-327-2842. You can see more of Scott's letters and learn a lot more about Illustrated Sales Letters in the free 12-Week Ultimate Sales Letter Course delivered by e-mail. Enroll at *www. Ultimate-Sales-Letter.com.*

Exhibit #23

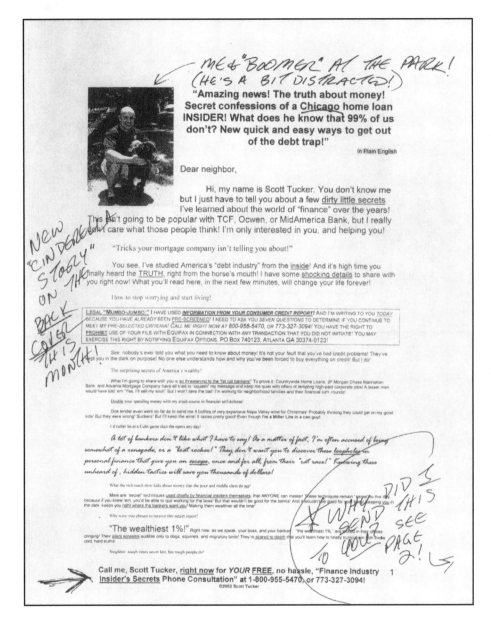

(Handwritten annotations on the image)

ME & "BOOMER" AT THE PARK! (HE'S A BIT DISTRACTED!)

NEW "CINDERELLA" STORY ON THE BACK COVER THIS MONTH!

DID I SEND THIS TO YOU? WHY? SEE PAGE 2!

"Amazing news! The truth about money! Secret confessions of a Chicago home loan INSIDER! What does he know that 99% of us don't? New quick and easy ways to get out of the debt trap!"

In Plain English

Dear neighbor,

Hi, my name is Scott Tucker. You don't know me but I just have to tell you about a few dirty little secrets I've learned about the world of "finance" over the years! This isn't going to be popular with TCF, Ocwen, or MidAmerica Bank, but I really don't care what those people think! I'm only interested in you, and helping you!

"Tricks your mortgage company isn't telling you about!"

You see, I've studied America's "debt industry" from the inside! And it's high time you finally heard the TRUTH, right from the horse's mouth! I have some shocking details to share with you right now! What you'll read here, in the next few minutes, will change your life forever!

How to stop worrying and start living!

LEGAL "MUMBO-JUMBO:" I HAVE USED *INFORMATION FROM YOUR CONSUMER CREDIT REPORT!* AND I'M WRITING TO YOU *TODAY* BECAUSE YOU HAVE *ALREADY* BEEN PRE-SCREENED! I NEED TO ASK YOU *SEVEN QUESTIONS* TO DETERMINE IF YOU CONTINUE TO MEET MY *PRE-SELECTED CRITERIA! CALL ME RIGHT NOW AT 800-955-5470,* OR 773-327-3094! YOU HAVE THE RIGHT TO PROHIBIT USE OF YOUR FILE WITH EQUIFAX IN CONNECTION WITH *ANY* TRANSACTION THAT YOU DID NOT INITIATE! YOU MAY EXERCISE THIS RIGHT BY NOTIFYING EQUIFAX OPTIONS, PO BOX 740123, ATLANTA GA 30374-0123!

See, nobody's ever told you what you need to know about money! It's not your fault that you've had credit problems! They've kept you in the dark on purpose! No one else understands how and why you've been forced to buy everything on credit! But I do!

The surprising secrets of America's wealthy!

What I'm going to share with you is so threatening to the "fat cat bankers!" To prove it, Countrywide Home Loans, JP Morgan Chase Manhattan Bank, and Advanta Mortgage Company have all tried to "squash" my message and keep me quiet with offers of tempting high-paid corporate jobs! A lesser man would have told 'em "Yes, I'll sell my soul!" But I won't take the bait! I'm working for neighborhood families and their financial turn rounds!

Double your spending money with my crash course in financial self-defense!

One lender even went so far as to send me 4 bottles of very expensive Napa Valley wine for Christmas! Probably thinking they could get on my good side! But they were wrong! Suckers! But I'll keep the wine! It tastes pretty good! Even though I'm a Miller Lite in a can guy!

I'd rather be at a Cubs game than the opera any day!

A lot of bankers don't like what I have to say! As a matter of fact, I'm often accused of being somewhat of a renegade, or a "boat rocker!" They don't want you to discover these loopholes in personal finance that give you an escape, once and for all, from their "rat race!" Knowing these unheard of, hidden tactics will save you thousands of dollars!

What the rich teach their kids about money that the poor and middle class do not!

Mine are "secret" techniques used chiefly by financial insiders themselves, that ANYONE can master! These techniques remain "secret" to this day, because if you knew 'em, you'd be able to quit working for the boss! But that wouldn't be good for the banks! And it wouldn't be good for you either keeping you in the dark keeps you right where the bankers want you! Making them wealthier all the time!

Why were you chosen to receive this secret report?

"The wealthiest 1%!" Right now, as we speak, your boss, and your banker, "the wealthiest 1%," are sitting in their offices cringing! Their silent screams audible only to dogs, squirrels, and migratory birds! They're scared to death that you'll learn how to finally trump them with these cold, hard truths!

Neighbor, tough times never last, but tough people do!

Call me, Scott Tucker, right now for YOUR FREE, no hassle, "Finance Industry Insider's Secrets Phone Consultation" at 1-800-955-5470, or 773-327-3094!

©2002 Scott Tucker

Exhibit #24

● Two months "breathing room!" Nothing to pay <u>anyone</u> for two months! Won't that feel great? Finally able to go on vacation! Go ahead and make a list *right now* of all the things you'll do with all that extra dough!

● I can even include your taxes and insurance! ← WHO ELSE DOES THAT WHEN YOU'VE GOT DAMAGED CREDIT?

Just look what your stars say

Today's Horoscopes

By Scott Tucker

Today's Birthday: You'll learn quickly today, with the help of a short bald white guy advising you on your finances! You'll save time, money, and effort by following his advice! Your birthday present? A free, no hassle "Finance Industry Insider's Secrets Phone Consultation" with Scott Tucker!

To get the advantage, check the day's rating: 10 is the easiest day, 0 the most challenging

Aries (March 21-April 19): Today is a 6. The good news is Venus is moving into your sign! That should make you luckier in money, provided you reach out to financial "renegades," like Scott Tucker, for help!

Taurus (April 20-May 20): Today is an 8. Why not try something different? **Take the easy way out!** Phone up Scott Tucker for a class in financial ass-kicking! You'll feel refreshed!

Gemini (May 21-June 21): Today is a 6. You like raking in the dough, but you're not that keen on shelling it out! Call Scott Tucker to learn how to keep more of your dough in your pocket! You'll prob'ly even get some cash!

Cancer (June 22-July 22): Today is a 7. You know who a perfect financial advisor match for you would be? A no B.S., make-things-happen type! Somebody who'll protect you! Like Scott Tucker! Call him today!

Leo (July 23-Aug. 22): Today is a 6. There's no time to worry about who said what to whom! It doesn't matter, because there's work to keep you busy! That, and there's work to be done to "right what's wrong" with your wallet! Call Scott Tucker for a fresh perspective!

Virgo (Aug. 23-Sept. 22): Today is an 8. The time to take action is today! You know the exact moment has arrived! It's time to pick up the phone and call Scott Tucker to see what he can do for *you!*

Libra (Sept. 23-Oct. 22): Today is a 6. Even if you don't know the answer to all your financial problems, you can still ask the only the person who really can help you, and ask him <u>quickly</u>! Call Scott Tucker right now!

Scorpio (Oct. 23-Nov. 21): Today is a 7. Are you contemplating a new project? Don't know quite how you'll do it? Start by spreading the work around! Lean on Scott Tucker for help!

Sagittarius (Nov. 22-Dec. 21): Today is a 6. You'd rather make your fortune through a winning lottery ticket than hours of backbreaking labor! And Scott Tucker is just the ticket! Call him *today!*

I'M A CAPRICORN! → **Capricorn (Dec. 22-Jan. 19):** Today is an 8. You're smart! You can set up your job to practically do itself! Now set up your finances to handle themselves as well! Call Scott Tucker today to put everything on "auto-pilot!"

Aquarius (Jan. 20-Feb. 18): Today is a 6. Don't let yourself be kept from doing anything! Something you don't quite understand is about to become clear when you call Scott Tucker today for financial help!

Pisces (Feb. 19-March 20): Today is a 7. Stick with what you know is right, even if you're in the minority! Call Scott Tucker today to see how much money he can save *you!*

Copyright © 2002, Scott Tucker

Who else wants an <u>up to 47% monthly debt reduction</u>? If you <u>don't</u> believe that I can do this for you too, then see Lorenzo and Luz Correa's confidential story! (on the back cover!) If you only did <u>half</u> as good as them, you'd still come out like a champ! (The Correa's were "skeptics" too, but they called me anyhow! Smart folks!)

All this being said, neighbor, I'm still afraid <u>you might not be ready</u>!

Is there anyone who **<u>I do NOT want</u>** to call me right now? YES! I do NOT want a single **<u>negative person</u>** to call me! <u>Life's too short</u>! And...

@$$h@1e$ need not apply! ← IF YOU'RE A JERK, GO KICK THE DOG, OR ARGUE WITH THE NEIGHBORS, BUT LEAVE ME OUT OF IT!

I do NOT want a single "sour-minded" person to call me! Are you mad at the world? Or maybe you have good reason to be! But I'm here to *help*, but not to serve as your personal punching bag! Anyhow, if you really do want help, can be nice and friendly, and will <u>deal with me honestly</u>, call me right now at 800-955-5470, or 773-327-3094!

Now our talk on the phone is 100% FREE! It doesn't cost you one red cent!

But, here's the deal... I need you to call me <u>immediately</u>, or risk me not being able to fit you in for a couple months! Neighbor, if you're *suffocating* under the *crushing* weight of mortgages, car notes, student loans, credit cards, and/or high rate finance company loans... I can help you!

So, Let's get started!

You know, when folks first call me, many of them seem suspicious of me! I get the "20 questions!" Like I'm some kind of "shadowy, mysterious figure!" That's just ridiculous! (I guess it's funny, really! So you might as well "ask away" when <u>you</u> call!)

The "Uni-Bomber" I'm <u>not</u>! (Don't worry, they already caught that guy!)

I don't pick up my mail from a "P.O. Box" wearing a hooded sweatshirt, fake beard, and dark sunglasses! I'm a <u>real person</u>! Just like you! "Scott Tucker" is my real name! <u>I live right here in Chicago</u>! We're probably neighbors! I've even run into folks I've helped at Home Depot, Dominick's, and that "German Fest" thing they have every summer in Lincoln Square!

"Make" hundreds more dollars "take-home" money every month, actually working *less* than you do right now!

Everyone I've helped in the past tells me that they're still as happy with me as they were months, even years, before! Did you <u>hate</u> the last refinancing thing you went through? I've heard some really <u>amazing stories</u> from folks over the years! One couple told me of a "Loan Officer" that actually wore a leopard-print silk shirt, unbuttoned to display his chest hair! All kinds of <u>fake gold jewelry</u>, and some kind of "gew" to "style" his hair that made a mess of everything!

Like a used car salesman nightmare! Slicker than a wet weasel on a linoleum floor! It takes all kinds! It would be funny if it weren't so true!

So many folks find themselves not getting what *they* want because the person "helping them" is only interested in helping himself! When dealing with these characters, we shouldn't be surprised with who *really* benefits! It's time to trust someone to help you who has <u>PROOF</u> that his clients are happy with him! (Just read Lorenzo and Luz Correa's shocking confidential story! (on the back cover!))

*WHAT DOES YOUR MORTGAGE COMPANY KNOW THAT YOU DON'T? (PAGE 4!) →

Call me, Scott Tucker, <u>right now</u> for *YOUR* <u>FREE</u>, no hassle, "Finance Industry <u>Insider's Secrets</u> Phone Consultation" at 1-800-955-5470, or 773-327-3094!

3

©2002 Scott Tucker

Exhibit #25

"TCF <u>refused</u> to help us! We thought no one could help! Then we *finally* gave up and called Scott Tucker, just like he'd been bugging us to do for the last 4 <u>years</u>!"

"Our old first and second mortgages were with TCF. Even though we had always paid them on time, they refused to help us like Scott Tucker did! TCF said they would be able to fuss around the edges and kinda help us, but what Scott Tucker was able to do for us beat TCF <u>hands down</u>! Scott managed to pay off <u>every</u> bill we had! He paid off Capital One Visa, *both* TCF mortgages, our car loan, gave the car title back to us <u>free and clear</u>...no more car payment! Scott even paid off our CitiFinancial loan that was at 20% interest! And now all the interest we pay with the lender Scott found for is 100% tax deductible! The car and credit cards were not! Now we just write it off at the end of the year! Just like those "fat cats" do! Scott even gave us $1,000.00 to pay off Aspire Visa, even though it didn't show on our credit report! He also paid off Elan Visa, ACB's credit card, and now *all* our credit cards are at <u>zero</u> balances! But Scott didn't make us cut 'em up...we can use 'em again if we want to! Now we save $273.54 <u>every</u> month! That saves us $3,242.48 a year! And we even got two months with <u>no bills to pay</u>, <u>saving us another $3,820.36</u> right away! Scott even paid our past due property taxes! That saved us $1,348.96! And Scott had promised us $10,000.00 cash for new bay windows, but got us <u>$27,200.98 in cash</u>! He really came through! And now our credit reports are cleaned up too! Thanks Scott! We don't know why we didn't call you years ago! You're alright, buddy!"

Lorenzo Correa
Bagel Packager, Entenmann's, Inc.
Age 58

Luz Correa
Machine Operator, Switchcraft, Inc.
Age 59

6059 W. Fletcher (Belmont & Austin)
Chicago IL 60634-5110

Thursday, May 30, 2002

Rewrite for Passion!
Edit for Clarity!

Here is yet another chance to rewrite your piece. This time the accent is on the passionate side of your offer.

How to Put Passion into Your Sales Letter

Sales letter writing is no place for pure, cold, hard logic, even if you are selling a logical proposition to presumably logical people. I don't care what business you're in or who your prospects or customers are; they buy by emotion and then justify their choice with logic. My speaking colleague, the famous sales trainer and motivational speaker Zig Ziglar, calls that "emotional logic."

Even in very technical fields, you do not find too many hard-core analytical personalities in sales positions. These "cold fish" just can't make it in selling. Most successful salespeople—even in highly technical fields—have amiable, friendly, enthusiastic personalities. They are "people people." This gives us valuable clues about the necessary personality of a sales letter.

"Cold fish" sales letters rarely work. The purely factual approach fails almost every time it's used. A sales letter needs an enthusiastic personality—and because it is ink on paper, not warm flesh and blood, the letter has to work harder at being enthusiastic. That means that what will seem overly expressive when you write it will still wind up understated when it's read.

No matter what people may think about their own attention spans or those of their prospects, the number one sin in marketing in general (and sales letter writing in particular) is being boring. The desirable opposite, I think, is being exciting, passionate, and even a little wild! Are you eager to pull the passion from within yourself—to channel it into your sales letter? Here's an exercise I suggest you try: Assume you're writing a letter to someone with whom you're having an illicit affair. In the letter, you're going to convince your lover—who is slightly more conservative than you are, but who has shown signs of having a wild side—to take an entire week off to be with you. You must convince the person to make some excuse to be away from work and responsibilities for that week, to take all the risks inherent in this action in order to sneak away to the Bahamas with you, where you will have free use of a friend's villa, right on the beach. Use as many pages as you like. (You've got a sales job and a half here!)

You can be bold, daring, even shocking. You can be poetic; you can be romantic; you can be colorful in your descriptions of the sun, the sea, the land, the stars, the breeze, the ocean smell. Where will you go? What will you do when you get there? Anticipate the objections and eliminate them as you go. Make huge promises! Create an overwhelming desire in your reader to go with you on that trip—no matter what the risk!

I conducted this exercise in a direct-marketing seminar once; everyone in the group was participating eagerly except for one man. He came up to me after the seminar and told me he'd had problems with the whole idea.

"First of all," he said, "I've been married to the same woman for thirty-eight years. In all that time, I haven't even thought about an affair.

And there's certainly nothing exciting about my relationship. Second, I own a specialty electronic-parts business. We sell parts to manufacturers of electronic products. Our business is boring and so is theirs. We talk to each other in part numbers. No romance there. I don't think this is for me."

As I quizzed him about his business, I found that his was one of about a dozen similar companies in this funny little industry, all pursuing the same clientele, in the same dull, dreary, traditional way. The only two things his customers supposedly cared about were price and reliable, on-time delivery.

I'm a little embarrassed to admit it, but I took this fellow out after the seminar to a rather raucous bar I know and popped a few drinks into him. I wanted to loosen him up, try to get his motor revving. I challenged him to come up with a passionate, lively sales letter to send to companies he didn't have as customers, and to send just 10 or 20 at a time.

He came back a couple of months later, the proud and happy creator of a marketing revolution in his once-dreary little industry. His sales letter was printed in red ink, on hot-pink paper, with the headline:

> **69 Things You Can Do After Work**
> **When You Are Absolutely Free Of Worry**
> **About Whether Or Not Your Part**
> **Will Arrive On Time Tomorrow.**

In the first paragraph, he quickly told the reader about his huge inventory, 24-hour-a-day ordering service, air-courier shipments, and guarantee of on-time delivery. The rest of the 3-page letter was, sure enough, devoted to a list of 69 things a worry-free manager might do with an evening. Some were funny; some were ordinary, but pleasant; some were outrageous; a few were a little "blue." Enclosed with the letter was a copy of his regular parts catalog with a huge hot-pink sticker affixed to the front: "BORING BUT NECESSARY."

"Well," he said proudly, "what do you think?"

What did I think? Frankly, I was afraid he was going to tell me a horror story about how he had mailed these things and been laughed out of town. But the truth was, he'd sent out 100 of these pink-and-red motivators, gotten 22 telephone calls from amused (and amazed) recipients, and received 18 separate first-time orders, all of which converted to long-term accounts. The campaign was worth more than $200,000.00 in new business to him that year.

Although his situation was unique, the episode introduces a valuable lesson about putting passion into a sales letter. No matter what your business may be, you can find something to get excited about. If you can't romanticize your product or service or its direct benefits, you've got to be able to create excitement out of the feelings of owning it or using it, or the enjoyment of the money or time it saves. Find something for the reader to get excited about! It doesn't matter what your topic is; there is a way to give your sales story a passion injection.

Consider the example in Exhibit #26.

Exhibit #26

WHEN ARE YOU DOING TO GET TIRED ENOUGH OF BEING IN DEBT TO DO SOMETHING ABOUT IT?

Dear Friend,

You're getting this letter because—incredibly—it's a matter of public record that you're in financial difficulty!!! I say "dear friend," because six years ago, I was where you are now . . . embarrassed. Frustrated. Hounded by creditors. Paranoid. Defensive. Angry. Wondering whether I'd ever get ahead. Hating the ring of the phone.

That experience motivated me to become a researcher. In one year, six years ago, I spent over 300 hours at the public library, at the law library, interviewing accountants and CPAs and tax experts and attorneys. From all that, I developed a nine-point step-by-step strategy for getting out of debt once and for all. It worked for me. I can work for you. Here are some of the nine steps:

1—STOP creditors' collection actions (in 90% of the cases, without bankruptcy, without an attorney!)

3—PROTECT your personal and family property from creditors

5—"DAMAGE CONTROL" for your credit rating and credit reports, so you can rebuild fast

7—Establish a spare time, weekend, 2nd income of $300 to $500 per month, from your choice of a dozen different proven plans

All nine of my steps can save your financial life!

My information will stop the wolves from barking at your door . . . protect your possessions . . . give you time to breathe and think . . . reorganize your payments to an amount you really can handle . . . put more money in your pocket . . . give you knowledge, control, confidence and peace of mind. How about a good night's sleep—for a change? Here I am, my friend . . . at the end of the tunnel . . . shining a beacon of light back toward you, saying "C'mon, let me help you escape your Debt Trap!"

Right now, you can hear all about my nine step system just by making a simple telephone call to 1-900-000-0000. I've recorded a message especially for you! You'll hear my personal debt-to-riches story . . . how my strategy works . . . and how you can get and try it yourself on a satisfaction guaranteed basis. There is a charge for the call: $2.00 for the first minute and $1.00 for each additional minute which will appear on your phone bill—but this is a very small cost to invest in getting debt free!

Aggressive Editing

Now that we've added a splash of color and passion, it's time to get a little ruthless with your text.

Aggressive editing means cutting out every word or phrase that fails to advance, strengthen, or reinforce your basic sales story. You're not editing to shorten. You are editing to clarify, and that will automatically shorten the letter.

For example, a sales letter draft had this wording:

We have many imitators, but no one who matches the quality of our products, our eight years of leadership in this industry, or our guarantee . . .

In the aggressive editing process, this was changed to:

Our many imitators can't match . . .

See how much faster that gets to the point? How much clearer it makes the letter?

This process takes days. You may need to attack your text, set the draft aside, then come back to it hours later and edit some more. But do it!

Compare Your Draft to Examples

I like to put my draft side by side with good examples, to compare and check for ways to improve my letter. This book is full of examples useful for this purpose.

Don't use just one letter for comparison—find several that allow you to isolate the strengths and weaknesses of your words.

Does your letter's text flow as smoothly as those of the comparison letters? Is it as compelling? Does it speak to its target audience as well? Is it structurally as sound? Is it as easy to understand? Does it excite a potential reader to action as effectively?

When you've spent a good chunk of time reviewing how your letter stands up to the others reproduced in this book, consider incorporating changes and revisions based on your observations.

Pretest

The draft developed in the privacy of your PC is ready for comments from the outside world. Turn on your office copier, pass the text around, and get ready for feedback!

No-Cost Pretesting

These days even a relatively small direct-mail test of, say, 5,000 to 10,000 units can cost a small fortune. That's why I like to pretest (at a cost of zero dollars, of course). I find glitches that can still be repaired before mailing, and get a better feel for the probable success or failure of the letter. In a few cases, the pretest feedback has been so bad that I've trashed the entire letter and started over. In most cases, nothing that drastic happens, but I do detect a few final opportunities for improvement.

The following are the best no-cost ways to pretest a sales letter.

1. Read the Letter Aloud

Your letter should flow smoothly, conversationally, whether read silently or aloud. If you find tongue twisters or hang-ups, fix them. The sales letter must read easily.

2. Read the Letter to Several People Who Might Be Typical Customers for the Offer

I know one highly paid copywriter of sales letters geared to blue-collar men. He routinely takes his letters down to a neighborhood bar, buys a round of beers for everybody, and then reads them his sales letter drafts. He welcomes their comments and ideas. But he's more interested in the secret acid test that they have no idea they're participating in. If some of them start asking how they can get the product or service described in the letter, he knows the basic approach is sound. If the letter is exciting enough to move people from the critic's corner to the cash-register line, he knows he's got a winner.

Sometimes this type of input can lead to dramatic results. I gave one client's direct-mail package—a short letter, a full-color catalog, and a response device—to a few typical customers; they looked through it all, but then they had a zillion questions! So the good news was that it got some motors running. The bad news was that it left lots of unanswered questions that could prevent response. As a result, I created a new 8-page sales letter that answered all of their questions. Response is up almost 15 percent since my client started using the new letter.

3. Have a Young Child Read the Letter Aloud to You

Any words or phrases that the youngster has difficulty with should probably be changed. I've used this strategy for many years; however, it is now more important than ever.

I know that many will instantly object to this idea. Perhaps you think your customers are "smarter than the average bear." If so, consider an article from *DM News* headlined: "Look Who's Opening Your Direct-Mail—And Can They Read It?" It reads, in part, as follows: "Over 27 million adults cannot read. An additional 46 million are either functionally illiterate or marginally illiterate. This means that one out of every three adult Americans lacks a skill level required to be satisfactorily literate in today's society."

Of course, the important question is: Are your customers literate? The article goes on: "Many marketing professionals feel that this incidence of illiteracy does not pertain to their own potential customers, particularly when mailing business-to-business. A word of caution: Illiteracy is not restricted to those standing in the unemployment lines. Sadly, perhaps, corporate America, in order to fill available job openings, has found it necessary to lower its employment requirements. Others who are illiterate have found ways to bypass the system and secure employment without detection."

It's my most current, admittedly curmudgeonly observation that the younger-than-30 crowd is even less literate, less intelligent, and cursed with poorer attention spans than are the rest of us. If you are writing to MTVers, you are writing to nonreaders.

I believe that mysterious failures of creatively and technically sound sales letters may very well be due, at least in part, to this large, growing, and somewhat hidden functional illiteracy. This is a strong mandate for lowest-common-denominator copywriting.

Beyond the straightforward illiteracy issue is what I call the Sophistication Trap: stubbornly believing that your customers are more sophisticated than they really are.

Some of the most talented, highly skilled, and best-paid copywriters on the planet create the full-page, copy-intensive direct-response ads that appear in the *National Enquirer* and similar tabloids. Some of these copywriters earn fees and royalties of $25,000.00 to $100,000.00 per ad. To command that kind of money, you just have to be good. And for an advertiser to pay that kind of money, there have to be outstanding results. So if you want to go to a school of profitable copywriting tutored by the best and the brightest, pick up a copy of the *National Enquirer*. Skip the articles about the invading Martians impregnating talk show hosts—but study the ads!

If you choose to stick with the bias that your customers are much smarter and more sophisticated than that, I believe that choice will cost you a great deal of money.

First of all, there are a lot of closet *National Enquirer* readers out there—just take a look at the circulation figures! Second, no matter who your customers are, they are part of the buying public that is reached and swayed by TV commercials, which are now geared to a sixth-grade reading level. Butcher, baker, candlestick maker, doctor, lawyer, CEO—they're all people who respond to the same basic motives and appeals. And the key word there is "basic." Regardless of who you are addressing your copy to, it is better to err on the side of simplicity. Bear in mind the famous remark attributed to P.T. Barnum: no one ever went broke overestimating the ignorance of the American public. Lots of people have gone broke overestimating the sophistication of their customers.

Bring Your Letter to Life

Finally—you're free to have your edited draft prepared exactly as you intend to send it out, on the typewriter, PC, or typesetting equipment. In other words, you can now pretend you are getting it ready for the printer. Think of this as your "dry run" or "dress rehearsal."

This is an exciting step because your letter comes to life before your eyes! What do you think of the current state of your project?

Change Graphic Enhancements

Meet with your typesetter, layout artist, and printer to discuss the graphic devices you've plugged in, and solicit their ideas.

This is also the time to work on the design of any enclosures going with the letter: coupons, certificates, product photos, or reply cards. Whatever you select, be absolutely certain that you like it, and that it appeals to your target readers. Changes after this stage are expensive and frustrating. Think twice.

Edit Again

Oops! Did you mean to write that? Wasn't the page break supposed to come farther down the sheet? Why did you choose to print the text in that hard-to-read color? What did you have in mind when you chose that typeface? Why is the headline hardly distinguishable from the rest of the letter?

This is a painful step. Nobody likes it. But you will notice things that you must change in this supposedly finished form, things that you missed previously. Bite the bullet and make the changes. You don't want anything less than a completely compelling sales letter.

Once you've accepted the idea of making these changes, it's probably as good a time as any to repeat Step 15, "Check the Checklists."

Mail a Mockup

Things seem to be all set. It's off to the printer, right?

Wrong.

Now is the time for you to put together the best mockup of the entire mailing that you can, with all of the enclosures, and then mail it to yourself. Your objective here is to receive it, see it, and handle it in the context of your normal stack of mail.

This may seem like a needlessly time-consuming chore, but it is perhaps the most important of the later steps. If your piece is of such a size that it will be roughed up and damaged by the post office, you should know that. If your piece does not compare well to the other mail you receive on an average day, you should know that. If your piece is meant to convey a "personalized" feeling, and it winds up looking like the rest of the "junk mail," you should know that.

You have worked too hard and spent too much time developing your letter to send it out without determining exactly how it will appear in its actual selling environment. Take the time to produce a mockup and mail it. Your prospective customers are likely to look much less charitably on the receipt of your letter than you do, but you will at least have something approaching a "real-life" test of your letter's initial appearance and effectiveness.

The Cool Off

You probably don't want to hear this, but the best thing for you to do once you receive your mockup is—nothing. At least for a few days. The reason? You need to win back some objectivity. That quality is probably in pretty short supply now.

The more you work with your sales letter, the more likely you are to fall in love with it—see its beauties but not its blemishes. Also, you're going to get impatient with this admittedly lengthy—but effective—system. For these reasons, a 3- to 5-day cooling-off period is a good idea.

I confess that I sometimes work under such intense deadline pressure that I skip this step, even several of these last steps; I think my finished work in those situations suffers a little as a result. However, I would welcome the luxury of extra time to restore my objective judgment. If you have the time, take the time.

Get Second Opinions

I believe in getting second opinions, within certain very definite limits. You may have gotten such opinions earlier in this process, as part of pre-testing. It won't hurt to get them again, now that you have done a great deal more work. The more experienced your contact, the better the advice is likely to be.

Getting an Expert Second Opinion

Who's an expert? Tough question. Everybody recognizes how unqualified everybody else is to opine on a matter, but no one considers himself unqualified to do so. (Consider that several surveys have shown that something close to 70 percent of all licensed drivers consider themselves "above average," which is a statistical impossibility!) There is certainly no shortage of available opinions. Unfortunately, most are at best worthless—and at worst, dangerous.

Many people in direct marketing develop their own little networks of peers and colleagues to bounce ideas, copy, and drafts off of in search of valid feedback. If you write a lot of sales letters, you need to develop such a network. If you don't know appropriate people, I'd suggest setting about meeting them. Seek out your local Direct Marketing Club and attend its meetings. Seek out your peers in national, state, and local trade associations who are aggressive, progressive marketers. And get a copy of the classic self-improvement book *Think and Grow Rich* by Napoleon Hill; study his ideas about forming a "mastermind group." There you'll find a little blueprint for your own creative alliance.

Of course, this book, too, has been designed to serve as a consultant to you and to provide guidance for your sales letter writing.

Finally, I'd like to offer you a little personal assistance. On the next page, you'll find one of my Critique Certificates, which entitles you to submit one printed piece—such as a sales letter—for your business, for my personal review and comment. We routinely charge no less than $200.00 per critique, so this is a very real $200.00 value. It's probably the only time in your life that you'll ever buy an inexpensive book and find $200.00 stuck inside it!

And it's very possible that redeeming it will prove even more valuable to you.

$200.00 CRITIQUE

$200.00 CERTIFICATE

Entitles bearer to submit any single printed piece; letter; brochure; catalog; direct-mail piece; advertisement; or similar promotional material by mail for critique by Dan S. Kennedy.

Name _____

Company (if any) _____

Address _____

_____

City, State, Zip _____

Phone _____ Fax _____

E-Mail Address _____

Send Certificate and Materials To:
Glazer-Kennedy Inner Circle, Inc.
407 West Pennsylvania Avenue
Towson, Maryland 21204

TERMS & CONDITIONS: Certificate expires 12 months from date of book purchase. Allow 6 to 8 weeks for Mr. Kennedy's response. Do NOT telephone; consultation given by mail only. Actual finished materials or "rough sketch" and copy for planned material may be submitted. Coupon redeemable only for listed services. Additional consulting may be contracted for, Mr. Kennedy's schedule permitting; fees quoted on request.

Please be advised that any materials submitted for review by Dan Kennedy, including those submitted with critique coupons, may be published in any of Dan Kennedy authored/edited publications, as examples. Also, submitted materials will not be returned. Do not submit materials you are concerned about keeping confidential. © 2005 D.S. Kennedy.

Code: USL05

Give It the Final Review

This is it—the last chance to tinker and tighten. Take the time to find a quiet, peaceful place and scrutinize your letter just one more time.

Go to Press

Give it to the printer—but don't give up control. Make sure your concept stays intact. If you're dealing with a complex mailing or a large quantity, check proofs and bluelines personally and carefully. Changes during this period—that is, from the time you hand over the mechanicals to the time you give the okay for the work to go on press—fall into two categories: printer errors (PEs) and author alterations (AAs).

After following the exhaustive review and double-check procedures outlined in this book, there's very little likelihood that you're going to decide to rewrite paragraphs now. But if you do, be prepared to pay—a lot. AAs are expensive, and you should only indulge in them if you find a glaring and damaging mistake. At this point, moving commas from inside the quotation marks to outside isn't the best use of your resources.

PEs, however, are another story. If you wanted yellow underlining and got a dull orange, make some noise and don't let the printer talk you into letting it go "as is." If the photos have uneven color values, tell the printer to go back and do the job again. If you selected a certain paper stock/color/size and are told it will be "easier for everybody" if you use what "everyone else uses," raise a stink about it. You're paying the bill. You're calling the shots. If the letter doesn't deliver, you will be the one to get hurt. Have it your way.

Of course, correcting PEs—errors arising from printer mistakes—should not cost you anything extra. Nevertheless, it is not uncommon for a few such items to sneak onto your bill once the job is complete. Printers do this to see if you are really paying attention. Don't let them down; show them that you are.

Mail!

At last—it's time to get your letters out the door. But before you do, take the time to ask yourself a few key questions. Most of the topics addressed here have probably been addressed in earlier steps—but if, once you review them, you find yourself reassessing, for instance, your list selection or your mailing method, you may want to make a change now.

Tips for Mailing to Special Groups

Who are you mailing to? And how? No one mailing approach is right for all audiences.

Narrow-Market Mailings

Some companies do many small-quantity mailings aimed at narrowly selected segments of their own customer or prospect lists. An office supply firm, for instance, might isolate only its customers who own PCs for a special offer on related supplies, an equipment upgrade, or a trade-in program. When conducting such highly specialized mailings (usually to fewer than a thousand recipients), you may find the ideas listed here helpful. Used properly, they can increase response tremendously.

Use Real Stamps, Not Metered Postage

Some pros even use commemorative stamps when possible. Stamps convey a personal feel; a metered imprint says, "mass mailing."

Type the Envelopes

You also could address them by hand. Or have ink-jet or computer imprinting done that perfectly mimics typewriting. Do not use labels unless absolutely unavoidable—and, if you do, then forget all about "sneaking up on 'em," and load up your envelope with bold teaser copy designed to compel the recipient to open it.

Use Rubber Stamps

A rubber-stamped imprint such as FIRST CLASS MAIL or URGENT! or REQUESTED INFORMATION ENCLOSED will deliver impact. This idea, like the first two, contributes a person-to-person look to the envelope that increases its likelihood of surviving the junk-mail sort—and whatever survives that "first cut" is a much better candidate to be opened and receive prompt attention.

Consider Nonpostal Delivery

UPS, Federal Express, messenger services, Western Union—all these delivery media have been used successfully with sales letters. While these methods are expensive, they are fast, reliable, and virtually guarantee that your letter gets to the right person, gets opened, and gets read.

Consider Innovative Packaging

You might opt for extra-bulky envelopes, bubble bags, boxes, tubes, or other "odd" packages or enclosed objects as a way of commanding attention. One campaign used cassette players inside stuffed toy bears, with an audiocassette sales message waiting for the recipient. The bears were delivered by courier to the prospects. Two hundred such deliveries were made; 140 responses came in; and the marketer eventually did business with more than 50 of the 200 prospects!

Success Tips for Big Mailings

There are many times when companies mail thousands, tens of thousands, even hundreds of thousands of units of a given mailing. With these quantities, the personalization techniques outlined here simply cannot be used.

Frankly, there are very few effective ways to enhance the effectiveness of such mailings—beyond, of course, writing the very best copy possible. However, there are a few tips you can follow.

Avoid Self-Defeating Address Designations

OCCUPANT. SALES MANAGER. POSTAL PATRON. When you see these or similar titles on your mail, what is your first reaction? If you're like most of us, the answer is simple: throw it away. This kind of addressing screams "junk mail!" The extra costs involved in actual name addressing usually represent a very good investment. If this is not practical for you, then try some imaginative addressing.

To the BUSY FAMILY that lives at
123 Cherry Hill Lane
Anytown, Ohio 00000

To the CONCERNED PARENTS living at 456 Main Street
Smallville, Vermont 00000

To the PERSON WHO MUST INCREASE SALES for
XYZ Enterprises, Inc.
123 Business Street
Metropolis, TX 00000

Use Strong Teaser Copy on the Envelope Exterior

If you cannot simulate the look of a personal letter with stamps, individual addressing, and so forth, you might as well go to the other extreme: openly and clearly "confessing" that you are writing with some kind of offer, and saying something that commands the attention and interest of the recipient.

Consider Using Celebrity Identification

Of course, this is not right for all mailings, but there are reasons why American Family Publishers uses Ed McMahon so prominently in its campaigns: to draw instant attention and lend a measure of recognition and credibility to the mailing piece. You too can hire an appropriate national or local celebrity and use the person's name and photo on your envelopes.

Different Weapons

Different targets require different weapons. Take the time to analyze your target carefully—to understand your customer. Then pick the best possible weapons and act decisively.

Congratulations!

These are the exact same 28 steps that I walk through every time I craft a new sales letter, and they are the same steps that I teach in my lectures and seminars on direct marketing. I sometimes call it a "miracle system" because I have seen many people with no formal training, background, or experience in advertising—and with minimal writing talent—sit down, follow these steps, and put together letters that get fantastic results. I know this system can work miracles for you, too!

I would add that the use of Ultimate Sales Letters should be incorporated in an Ultimate Marketing Plan. What is an Ultimate Marketing Plan? I'm very glad you asked! Such a Plan begins with a triangle: Message, Market, Media. Sales letters are, in many cases, the best Media weapon. In almost every case they are a Media weapon that should be employed. But media should never be considered out of context of the other two parts of the triangle. In fact, media is usually the wrong place to start. You can get comprehensive assistance in developing your own Ultimate Marketing Plan in my book of that title, and in a separate 12-week Course delivered by e-mail, free of charge, for purchasers of that book.

The Most Versatile
Sales Tool of All

Now that you've learned the Ultimate Sales Letter system and have it at your disposal, you'll want to get the maximum value from it. There are eight major ways we can use these kinds of sales letters for our own businesses and for clients. We'll look at each one in this section.

1. To Create Qualified Leads

In-person cold calling has become prohibitively expensive and leads to high sales-force turnover. Cold-call telemarketing is also expensive and discouraging to telemarketers. Salespeople need qualified leads—it's that simple!

Once a good sales letter is developed and proved effective in generating qualified leads for your salespeople, you have the most controllable, manageable, and predictable lead generator in existence. There are, of course, many other ways to generate leads. Trade shows or mall exhibits work, but they produce huge surges of leads in a few days, not a consistent flow. Media advertising of one kind or another can be used to provide leads, but results will vary tremendously based on all sorts of uncontrollable factors: day of the week, position on a page, the TV program running opposite your commercial, and so on.

A letter campaign that reliably produces, say, three leads per hundred units mailed will just about always produce at that level. The inherent variables of other media do not interfere with a letter campaign.

When someone picks up the phone and calls you in response to your sales letter, you know you've probably got a qualified prospect!

2. To Support Telemarketing

Many businesses with active outbound telemarketing operations find that sending a sales letter, then following up with the telephone call, works much better than a cold telephone call by itself. The letter paves the way. It gives the telemarketer a reason for calling. It provides the interested prospect with reference information to refer to during the conversation.

This works whether the purpose of the phone call is to make an appointment or to make a sale.

A good example of this kind of letter appears as Exhibit #27 (on page 170).

3. To Create Store Traffic

There's a Cadillac dealer in our area who mails a sales letter to me at least once a month, announcing some type of sale or event going on at the dealership. (I assume I'm on the list by virtue of owning a Lincoln Continental and/or living in a certain Zip Code.) These letters are designed to create traffic to the dealership. They are obviously working or I wouldn't keep getting them. Just about any retail business could certainly copy and use such an approach.

I know of one occasion when this kind of sales letter campaign actually built a business from scratch. A deli and restaurant targeted all of the offices and businesses nearby, including many offices in high-rise towers, and used a sales letter to reach them. I don't have access to that letter anymore, but it went something like this:

WHO SAYS THERE'S NO SUCH THING AS A FREE LUNCH?

To introduce you to our huge, delicious sandwiches made to order with fresh deli meats and imported cheeses, we're going to give you a free lunch—no strings attached—no other purchase necessary. Come by yourself, bring the whole gang—from now until April 1, everybody gets a free sandwich!

The letter then continued with several short paragraphs describing the deli's specialty sandwiches, locations, hours, and credit cards honored.

Of course, people bought drinks, side salads, and desserts, and the profit on those items helped offset the true cost of the free sandwiches. And the owner calculated that "buying his clientele" for a couple of months this way would be faster and cheaper than a longer-term commitment to all sorts of media advertising. He was right. By the time he had mailed only 300 letters, he had given away nearly twice that many sandwiches—and had satisfied enough people that his repeat business every day jammed that little restaurant to its seams.

Exhibit #27

"A money-saving message exclusively for small company CEOs . . ."

Dear Beleaguered Business Owner,

I say "beleaguered" because I know you are surrounded by taxes—payroll taxes, income taxes, sales taxes, taxes, taxes and more taxes!!! Well, I have some incredibly good news for you:

In the last 6 months, right here in (name of city), our company has helped 164 businesses reduce their property taxes. We've helped more than 100 even get rebates! We believe we can do the same for you.

Best of all, there is no charge for our service—unless and until we put money in your bank account!

It will take me less than 30 minutes to . . .

1. Explain this service and our other business services to you

2. Look at just four statistics in your financial statements, to determine the probability of us saving you money

One of my associates will be calling you in the next few days to arrange an appointment that is convenient for you. Please ask your receptionist or secretary to put through the call from DOLLAR-SAVERS INC., so we can get together soon.

Thank you,

John Q. Dollar

John Q. Dollar
President
Dollar-Savers, Inc.

P.S. Remember—the sooner we get to talk to you, the sooner we can work to reduce your tax burden!

---

4. To Stimulate Referrals

This is an underused category of sales letter that I find particularly fascinating. I teach marketing techniques to dentists and chiropractors throughout the United States and Canada and have devised many referral-stimulation letters for their use. Most of my clients get very good results from using them. You can see two examples of such letters in Exhibits #28 and #29 (pages 172 and 173).

Exhibit #28

Mr. Dan Kennedy
5515 N. 7th Street
Phoenix, AZ 85014

Dear Mr. Kennedy:

We've come up with a great way to treat your friends as well as yourself.

Just give the coupons below to two friends or business associates who haven't yet tried Courtyard. Each coupon entitles them to a free weekend night at any Courtyard Hotel just for spending one night with us. Now that's a sure way to win friends overnight.

And there's more. Once a coupon is used by a new Courtyard guest, we'll send you a voucher in return that's good for a half-price night. So if both coupons are used, you also get a free night.

It's our way of thanking you for introducing your fellow business travelers to all the features Courtyard has to offer. From the spacious rooms and king-size beds to the whirlpool and friendly staff. You know from experience that Courtyard is always ready to make everyone's stay a pleasure.

And with this offer, we're also ready to make it free. The attached coupons, which can only be used by someone other than yourself, are good through December 30, 2004. And the vouchers you receive in return are valid through April 1, 2005.

So tear off the coupons now and give them away.

Of course, you've now come to the only problem with this offer: who are you going to give them to? Have fun deciding!

Sincerely,

Brent Andrus

Brent Andrus
V.P., Marketing and Sales

Detach coupons here and give them to two friends.

To redeem, stay one night and present this coupon at check-in for your free weekend night voucher. Call for exact locations and reservations 1-800-321-2211	To redeem, stay one night and present this coupon at check-in for your free weekend night voucher. Call for exact locations and reservations 1-800-321-2211
Exclusively for the friends and associates of: Mr. D. Kennedy 272543104 *USED BY:* Name (PLEASE PRINT) _____ Address _____	*Exclusively for the friends and associates of:* Mr. D. Kennedy 272543104 *USED BY:* Name (PLEASE PRINT) _____ Address _____
Redeem before 12/30/04; only one coupon per stay. Free weekend night must be taken by 4/1/05, rooms offered are standard Courtyard rooms and subject to availability. Does not apply with other offers and discounts. No coupon facsimiles accepted.	Redeem before 12/30/04; only one coupon per stay. Free weekend night must be taken by 4/1/05, rooms offered are standard Courtyard rooms and subject to availability. Does not apply with other offers and discounts. No coupon facsimiles accepted.

Reprinted courtesy of Marriott Courtyard.

Exhibit #29

DIRECT MARKETING ASSOCIATION, INC.
6 East 43rd Street * New York, NY 10017 * 212-555-4077

Dear DMA Member:

I'd like to ask you to look through your Rolodex or address book and come up with the name of at least one person who probably isn't a DMA member, but who you believe should be.

You see, we're embarking on a new membership enrollment campaign at the DMA. And the logical place to start is with you. I know that you have many contacts both in and outside the direct marketing industry. And you know what DMA does for you and your counterparts in all kinds of direct marketing organizations who use direct marketing techniques. Surely, you know someone who would benefit from DMA membership but who for one reason or another may not be aware of what the DMA has to offer. And, if you can help us build the number of people in your segment, we'll be able to offer even more services to you.

I'd appreciate it if you'd send that person's name, address and phone number to me. Because I'd like to talk to him or her about joining the DMA before the year is up.

For your convenience, I've enclosed a form on which you can list the name of your nominee. I'd also like to know if you'd permit me to use your name when I make the actual contact. So I've included a check-off box to that effect on the form as well. Obviously, we will respect your wishes.

I appreciate your taking the time from your busy schedule to help us. I look forward to receiving your nomination and soon hope to add your referral to our membership roles.

Sincerely,

Michael Faulkner

Michael Faulkner
Vice President
Membership Development

P.S. You may wish to consider an associate who is presently not in direct marketing or who may only be using it to a limited extent. As our industry grows, they are among those people most likely to need our services.

Reprinted courtesy of Direct Marketing Associates, Inc.

5. To Introduce New Products or Services to Present or Past Clients

If there is one universal discovery I've made with every business I've ever consulted with—small or large, local or global, industrial or consumer-targeted, product or service-oriented—it is that they all underutilize their own customer mailing lists. (Some don't even maintain such a list!)

I have a simple premise and a simpler method for increasing just about any business's sales through the use of sales letters. First, the premise: It is easier to sell more to customers who know you, like you, and trust you than it is to get more new customers. The first sale is the toughest; the established customer is predisposed to purchase from you again. Second, the method: Develop and mail a new sales letter to all of your customers each and every month, introducing a new product or service.

Let me point out, by the way, that if a product or service is new to the customer, it's new, period. I have one client who sells a variety of products to hospitals and clinics. We broke down his customer lists by what people had bought and what they hadn't bought. Even though he sells about a hundred different items, most customers were buyers of only three or four. So we created a complex program of single-product sales letters sent to nonbuyers of those products. If you bought Product A, you got a letter about a product you hadn't bought—say, Product B. But if you were a user of B and had never bought A, you got the letter about A. These letters have been consistently pulling a 2 to 3 percent order rate and averaging $1.00 of gross profit per letter mailed. Think about that! If every sales letter you mail reliably brings back at least $1.00 of profit, what do you do? Right—mail as many as you can!

6. To Sell Directly by Mail Order

Yes, mail order is a huge subject in and of itself that cannot be covered here. I would only like to point out that many non–mail order firms can still generate some business purely through sales letters.

Earlier in this book I showed you how a Las Vegas hotel marketed "vacation packages" via sales letters.

If you have regular, repeat customers, there's probably a way for you to obtain reorders and stimulate additional purchases from them with periodic sales letters.

An example of an "ordinary business" using a sales letter to sell directly by mail appears as Exhibit #30.

Exhibit #30

THE PET FOOD SUPERSTORE
123 Dog Street
City, State, Zip

Dear Customer,

SAVE 50% ON NEW SUPER-ANTI-TICK SHAMPOO JUST RIGHT FOR THE COMING SUMMER SEASON

We appreciate your business; we appreciate having you as a customer! Now, thanks to a special arrangement with the DOG CARE PRODUCTS COMPANY, we have an opportunity to say "Thanks!" with a very special, timely offer:

The enclosed brochure fully explains DOG CARE'S new SUPER-ANTI-TICK SHAMPOO and ANTI-TICK COLLAR products. You'll do your dog and your family a favor by putting these products to use before the start of the summer tick season, in just a few weeks. Right now, you can get a ½-quart bottle of the Shampoo and the Collar at half-price . . . you save $9.95! . . . you pay only $9.95. And you can order by mail or phone, and use your Visa or MasterCard if you like. We'll set the products aside here at the store for you or we'll ship them out, right to your door at no extra charge!

Call us today at 258-DOGG!

Your Friends At The Superstore!

7. To Reduce Refunds via Post-Purchase Reassurance

Salespeople are familiar with "buyer's remorse": A person may buy something on impulse, then a day or two later begin to feel bad about the purchase. Maybe the product isn't exactly what the buyer thought it was; maybe the problem has nothing to do with the product but a lot to do with having spent the money. Regardless of the reason, buyer's remorse can lead to refunds.

A good sales letter—with a congratulatory theme—sent to the customer the day after the purchase can make the sale stick.

Exhibit #31 is an example of such a letter, developed for a self-improvement program sold via cable TV. This letter, sent separately from the product, significantly reduced returns. Couldn't the same type of letter help with any product, service, or transaction that might be subject to buyer's remorse?

8. For All Sorts of Business and Personal Correspondence and Communication

We spend the lion's share of our lives selling! You have to sell yourself and your ideas to superiors, subordinates, associates, stockholders, vendors, and countless others every day. Actually, very little communication takes place without the intent of persuading.

Whether you need to write a letter to a customer or a supplier, to your stockholders, to the banker, to your son's or daughter's school principal, or to your senator, you'll be attempting to sell at least a viewpoint, if not something significantly more tangible than that.

The principles behind the system, then, apply to every type of persuasive communication. Studied and used, these techniques will make you a much more effective communicator.

Exhibit #31

Hello again!

By now you should already be deeply involved in your **THINK AND GROW RICH SUCCESS SYSTEM.** So I wanted to write and add my personal words of encouragement—and issue you a special challenge.

First, let me re-emphasize: I believe you now have the very best program of its kind in existence. By listening to the audiocassettes repeatedly (as you commute to and from work, for example), you'll find yourself automatically "getting in tune" with the thinking, the attitudes, the convictions necessary to win big in life! And by studying the book and utilizing the other course materials as directed, you'll master the principles and discover Napoleon Hill's great success secret that much sooner.

Let me also encourage you to give some time to studying your bonus **THINK AND GROW RICH** Business Reports and listening to the accompanying audiocassettes, which were prepared exclusively for you. Whether you want to start a business from scratch, buy a going business, buy a franchise, or more effectively promote your present enterprise, these reports provide "nuts and bolts" information you can put to work right now. Even if you don't yet see yourself as an entrepreneur, you can use the guidelines in the report on Winning Career Strategies to begin moving ahead. And the report entitled How to Gain Control of Your Finances may well be worth the entire price of admission!

Altogether, this system gives you a winning game plan. So now—as my coaches used to tell me—all you've got to do is execute! And that brings me to the second thing I wanted to talk with you about: the temptation to quit.

Even though this **THINK AND GROW RICH SUCCESS SYSTEM** has been wonderfully designed to help you master the principles as easily as possible, it still requires some dedication and persistent effort on your part.

Do you remember the old bromide, "Quitters never win and winners never quit?" Well, with that in mind, I'm going to say something now

Exhibit #31 (continued)

---

that may shock you: we're all quitters! And the sooner we realize it, the better. Then we can get on with the business of overcoming it.

Let me tell you about the time I quit.

It was in my next-to-last year in football, the 1977–78 season. With me as quarterback the year before, the Vikings had lost their third Super Bowl. The Minnesota fans had decided that Tarkenton had to go. People came up to me on the streets and in restaurants to tell me just that!

Our third game of the new season was against the Tampa Bay Buccaneers, then a two-year-old expansion team that had lost every game the previous year. Now they were in Minnesota playing the mighty Vikings, but we were losing in the fourth quarter!

Our great team had gotten a little older. We were struggling. In that fourth quarter, I think all 47,000 people in the stadium stood up and booed me. I'll never forget that day. I had suffered some mighty booing during my final season with the New York Giants in 1971, but nothing hurt as much as the sound of those Viking fans calling for my head on a platter. I came off the field that day more depressed and angry than I had ever been.

The next morning I walked into Coach Bud Grant's office and said, "I'm going home to Atlanta and I'm not coming back." I was quitting after the third game of the season.

The next day Bud called me in Atlanta. I said, "I've thought about it and I'm still quitting."

Bud Replied, "Fran, I wish I had some magic word to tell you that would make you come back and play. But I don't. I just hope you understand that if you don't come back, we have no chance to make the playoffs this year."

Now that really hit me!

I thought to myself, "You selfish son of a gun! Here you have 44 teammates out there. Old Tinglehoff and Marshall are up there busting their backsides. They're old and tired and they're still trying. But

---

Exhibit #31 (continued)

just because you get booed, you're going to run off and throw their chances to the wolves."

After I hung up, I packed my bags, got the next plane back to Minneapolis, and never said a word to anyone. I just showed up for Wednesday practice. Most people never knew I had quit.

The important thing to recognize is that winners are people who sometimes have the desire to quit, but *they develop ways of dealing with it.* And that's what **THINK AND GROW RICH** is all about.

Why have I told you this story?

Because you'll probably be tempted to quit, too. Maybe you'll listen to the tapes for a little while and not see any miraculous changes in your life, so you'll feel like quitting. Sometimes we're a little too "instant"-oriented these days. Maybe you'll try some new venture and "get your nose bloodied," and feel like quitting. I want you to know that, as far as I'm concerned, it's perfectly okay to feel like quitting now and then—as long as you don't!

I really want to see you take this winning **THINK AND GROW RICH** game plan and execute! That's why I'm excited about offering you this little challenge and reward:

Whenever you're ready, send in a list of the 25 most valuable ideas you've gained from your study of this THINK AND GROW RICH SYSTEM. Tell us how you've benefited from these ideas. We'll then send you a suitable-for-framing Certificate of Completion with Dr. Napoleon Hill's picture and his famous quotation, "Anything the mind can conceive and believe, it can achieve"; my photograph; and the signatures of myself and Mr. W. Clement Stone, the president of the Napoleon Hill Foundation.

I hope you'll be proud to hang this beautiful certificate in a prominent place in your home or office, where you'll see it often and be reminded that anything you can conceive and believe, you can achieve.

In closing, let me congratulate you once again on investing in this tested and proven program of self-development and achievement.

Exhibit #31 (concluded)

Believe me, I meet people all the time who wish for greater success, but I meet far fewer who, like you, are willing to do something about it.

Sincerely,

Fran Tarkenton

Fran Tarkenton

P.S. I've enclosed, as an extra gift from the publisher, two 25% discount certificates. Each may be used toward the purchase of any of the other fine programs offered in the **THINK AND GROW RICH BUSINESS REPORTS.** To me, winning is a daily proposition, something you're always learning to do better. For this reason, you'll undoubtedly want to add some of these other excellent programs to your success library.

The Million-Dollar Sales Letter Secret: The Power of a Sequence

One of the biggest mistakes most marketers make is doing "one-shot mailings." Simply put, it takes repetition to have impact. But I advise against Madison Avenue's extraordinarily slow, patient, plodding, expensive version of repetition, with results sloppily measured by market-share movement or brand recognition over long periods of time. Instead, I most often work with a tight, timed sequence over a 45- to 60-day period that is capable of quickly creating brand/message recognition as well as considerable, immediate response.

In this section, you'll see a series of my sales letters (Exhibits #32 and #33 on pages 184-187) for a chain of Italian restaurants that has literally become famous. I've used this series in all of my seminars for nearly 20 years, and shown it to well over 4 million people. For years, the only way to get this "model" was in my Magnetic Marketing System, for $399.00 or more. Not only do these letters include many of the tactics presented throughout this book, but they demonstrate how to structure a multistep mailing sequence. After you read these sample letters, ask yourself this simple question: Do you have any doubt that, in any household receiving these letters, Giorgio's is a topic of conversation?

Of course, people who sell "sophisticated" stuff to "sophisticated" people will quickly insist that they could never use something like this. They're very wrong. You *can* separate style from structure. The humorous style helps whether selling million-dollar computer systems to CEOs in the boardroom or carpet cleaning to folks in their living rooms. But the structure is absolutely proven to be universally effective. Often, the response from the second and third letters combined will double the response obtained from the first. Sometimes, it will even do better.

I call this my "million-dollar secret" because the creation of sales letter *sequences* rather than just creating sales letters is as responsible as any other single idea for my becoming a millionaire while still young enough to enjoy it, and for making millions and millions of dollars for my personal clients. As secrets go, I suppose it's not much of one. Frankly, I "stole" it from the collection industry; the Giorgio's letters, for example, are very closely modeled after a basic sequence of dunning letters—first notice, second notice, third notice. But very, very few marketers know to use this tactic or have the discipline to use it, so it's just as valuable as a bona fide secret.

Using the Power of Sequence after Sales Presentations

My Gold/VIP Member, Kevin Fayle, a marketing consultant to kitchen dealers and remodelers, tells his coaching group members to utilize the power of sequence mailings *after* a potential customer visits their stores or showrooms and leaves without buying. He urges the dealers to use sequence mailings during the often lengthy process of moving a customer from interest, through design decisions, to placing an order.

This again demonstrates the versatility of sales letters. While it's natural to think of them as a tool for getting an appointment, getting a prospect into a store, or even making a sale, they are also useful to follow up with unconverted prospects, to reactivate old, inactive customers, and to introduce new products to present customers. In every case, results improve with a sequence as opposed to just one letter.

Exhibit #32

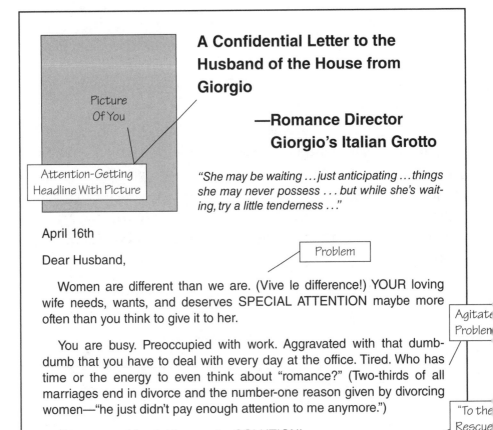

A Confidential Letter to the Husband of the House from Giorgio

—Romance Director Giorgio's Italian Grotto

Picture Of You

Attention-Getting Headline With Picture

"She may be waiting ... just anticipating ... things she may never possess ... but while she's waiting, try a little tenderness ..."

April 16th

Dear Husband,

Problem

Women are different than we are. (Vive le difference!) YOUR loving wife needs, wants, and deserves SPECIAL ATTENTION maybe more often than you think to give it to her.

Agitate Problem

You are busy. Preoccupied with work. Aggravated with that dumb-dumb that you have to deal with every day at the office. Tired. Who has time or the energy to even think about "romance?" (Two-thirds of all marriages end in divorce and the number-one reason given by divorcing women—"he just didn't pay enough attention to me anymore.")

For you, my friend, I have got a SOLUTION!

"To the Rescue" Solution

With this letter, YOU are entitled to an evening charmed by all the creativity of Giorgio, the Official Romance Director!

When you and your Very-Significant-Other arrive at Giorgio's, you'll be ushered to the special dining room lit only by candlelight and the roaring fire in the fireplace ... with the view of the sunset or starry night over the harbor! (When you make your reservation, I will GUARANTEE your choice of a near-the-fireplace or window-side table!)

Create Vivid Word Picture that Appeal to the Senses

In this undercrowded, intimate dining room there will be NO families, NO CHILDREN, NO disruptions. Quiet mood music. A peaceful environment. A haven from the hustle, bustle, noise, and pushing and shoving and rushing of the real world.

On your table, in a crystal bud vase, there will be a single dewy-fresh red rose for your lady. (It and the vase are hers to take home.)

We will begin with a carafe of our wonderful house Italian wine—red or white, your choice—compliments of Giorgio! And fresh baked, piping hot, lightly garlic-buttered, crusty Italian breadsticks.

For dinner, all the TENDERNESS the two of you can handle—if you choose the specialty of the house: an entrée of melt-in-your-mouth tender veal on a bed of angel hair pasta, with a to-die-for pesto sauce . . . or your choice of five other wonderful entrees.

Any choice from our dessert tray . . .

Espresso . . .

> Really Make Them See, Smell, and Taste It!

And finally a heart-shaped box with four delicate, Italian gelato filled chocolates presented to your lady with a flourish!

Now, is that an evening to enjoy, to luxuriate in, to remember? Will that make you a hero? Ah—Giorgio GUARANTEES it.

We can only accommodate twelve couples each evening with this very special Romance Dinner, so it's important to call and make reservations as early as you can. Ask for me—Giorgio—Noon to 10:00 p.m. (or stop in for our Businessman's lunch). See me, and make these Romance arrangements personally. I'm the handsome-looking devil in the deep blue tuxedo jacket, in the lounge.

Awaiting your commands—to make 'a magic for you!

> Limited Number Available

Giorgio.

P.S. The cost? EVERYTHING, the entire Romance Dinner for two exactly as I've described it—just $59.95. If you wish you can even pay in advance with VISA, MASTERCARD, AMERICAN EXPRESS, or CARTE BLANCHE and not be troubled by a check the evening you are here.

Exhibit #33

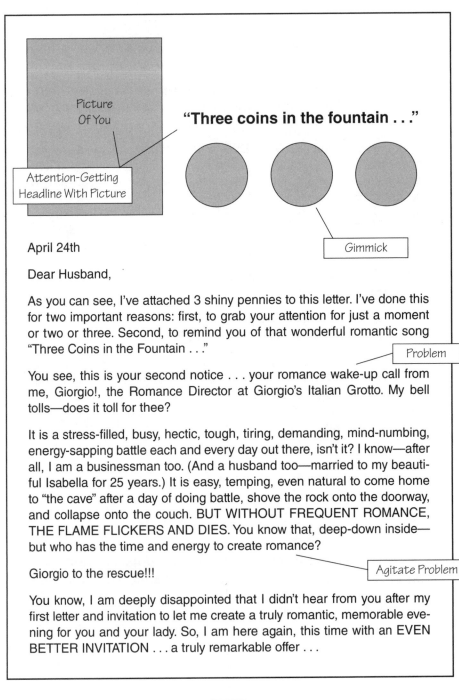

Picture Of You

Attention-Getting Headline With Picture

"Three coins in the fountain . . ."

Gimmick

April 24th

Dear Husband,

As you can see, I've attached 3 shiny pennies to this letter. I've done this for two important reasons: first, to grab your attention for just a moment or two or three. Second, to remind you of that wonderful romantic song "Three Coins in the Fountain . . ."

Problem

You see, this is your second notice . . . your romance wake-up call from me, Giorgio!, the Romance Director at Giorgio's Italian Grotto. My bell tolls—does it toll for thee?

It is a stress-filled, busy, hectic, tough, tiring, demanding, mind-numbing, energy-sapping battle each and every day out there, isn't it? I know—after all, I am a businessman too. (And a husband too—married to my beautiful Isabella for 25 years.) It is easy, temping, even natural to come home to "the cave" after a day of doing battle, shove the rock onto the doorway, and collapse onto the couch. BUT WITHOUT FREQUENT ROMANCE, THE FLAME FLICKERS AND DIES. You know that, deep-down inside—but who has the time and energy to create romance?

Giorgio to the rescue!!!

Agitate Problem

You know, I am deeply disappointed that I didn't hear from you after my first letter and invitation to let me create a truly romantic, memorable evening for you and your lady. So, I am here again, this time with an EVEN BETTER INVITATION . . . a truly remarkable offer . . .

For just $59.95, I will give you everything I described before, the romantic Dinner For Two—listed again, at the bottom of this letter—AND I WILL EVEN SEND A "STRETCH," GLEAMING WHITE, FULLY-EQUIPPED, LIMOUSINE RIGHT TO YOUR HOME to pick YOU—the "Prince" and your "Princess" up—and bring you home at the end of the evening! (Imagine the look in her eyes when you walk out the door and, instead of going to the garage, your tuxedoed chauffeur steps forward and opens the door of the limousine for your lady to enter!)

Irresistible Offer

If you say "no" to this invitation—ah, is there no romance in your heart? How can this be?

Call ME, Giorgio!, right now. I'm ready to make 'a magic for you!

Giorgio.
With a song in his heart.

HERE IS EVERYTHING INCLUDED FOR THE INCREDIBLE LOW PRICE OF JUST $59.95:

"High-Tech" Sales Letters

When I wrote the first edition of this book in 1991, very few marketers were using broadcast fax or fax-on-demand, and Internet sites, auto-responders, and e-mail were unknowns. Since then, of course, virtually every office and many homes have been equipped with fax machines. Millions of people use the Internet. E-commerce is rapidly growing. All of this prompts plenty of questions about how my Ultimate Sales Letter Techniques apply to these high-tech media. Fortunately, the answer is: very well!

1. The Fax Machine

In recent years, "broadcast fax"—mass faxing—became a very popular and, quite often, very effective marketing tool. Just for example, I developed a complete campaign of sales letters delivered by fax for a client who sells term life insurance to doctors, architects, airline pilots, and other specialized prospect groups—and we were selling millions of dollars of life insurance with no salespeople and no telemarketing. Unfortunately, broadcast fax to "cold" prospects with whom you have no relationship has basically been outlawed. Now, you may fax where a relationship exists, although the trend is toward an even higher standard: permission. For my businesses and my clients' businesses, we now incorporate language into order forms, enrollment forms, and other documents giving us permission to communicate with customers and prospects via fax, e-mail, and phone. This book is not legal advice, and it's up to you to determine which laws affect you and your business. However, you should know that sales letters sent by fax to customers or prospects offer many advantages: speed, low cost, and high impact.

For most purposes, faxed sales letters need to be kept to only one or two pages, and thus are best used to generate leads, not to make sales or even to secure appointments. But other than restricting the length, every suggestion, tactic, and example presented in this book—from what I said about headlines all the way through to what I said about ease of response—applies perfectly to the sales letter prepared for delivery by fax.

2. Fax-On-Demand

This is simply an automated way of delivering sales letters and other literature to prospects or customers requesting them, with no delay, no handling, and no printing and postage costs. Here, there are no real length limitations, any more than there are with sales letters delivered by mail. The drawback is that you can't use colors, photos may not fax clearly, you can't vary the size, color, and texture of the paper, and so forth. The advantages are speed and cost. In many instances, the tradeoff is acceptable. And again, every single guideline presented in this book applies to the sales letters you would store in a fax-on-demand (FOD) system, for delivery when requested. Many of the uses of FOD have moved to the Internet, with Web sites and auto-responder e-mail. However, I still have clients who use FOD successfully.

3. Internet Sites

You certainly can put even a lengthy sales letter up on a Web site and have it work for you there, and/or it can be downloaded by interested prospects. Among other things you'll find at my Web site, *www.Ultimate-Sales-Letter.com*, is the complete sales letter for my *No B.S. Marketing Letter* and Inner Circle Membership, which works very well. You do not need to fear "long copy" here any more than in printed pieces; seriously interested prospects want a lot of information.

Effective Web site design is a complex topic—and something most Web site designers are incredibly inept at! At the very end of this section, you'll find a brief dissertation on Web site copy from my Platinum Member Corey Rudl, a hugely successful Internet marketer. The Internet Marketing Center, the company Corey created, generates more than $40 million each year entirely through Internet marketing, and provides Internet marketing coaching to hundreds of business owners each month.

4. Auto-responders

This technology is somewhat similar to fax-on-demand. Web site visitors can request and have information sent to them computer-to-computer. You can also preprogram the sending of a sequence of e-mails; for example, 24 hours, then 72 hours, then 5, 10, and 15 days after a prospect has visited your site, all done for you—"look Ma, no hands!"

5. E-mail

If you are sending a requested sales letter via e-mail, length is still not an issue. If you're sending unasked-for follow-up e-mails, as I just described, brevity is required. The best technique I know is a brief e-mail giving the prospect a reason to return to the Web site for newly posted information—then do your selling there.

It's important to remember that most of the sales letter strategies presented in this book apply even to these brief e-mails. For example, the "RE" line on the e-mail should be a compelling headline.

My good friend Ken McCarthy was one of the earliest users of e-mail sales letters. He was even hired by leading Japanese technology companies to teach them how to use their own technology to sell via e-mail. He is a consistently reliable, sane, truthful voice in the confusing world of Internet marketing. Here is some of his basic advice about using e-mail for sales purposes:

"Good news: e-mail is cheap, fast and easy to use. Bad news: it's coming under increasing government regulation and industry self-regulation. So, Rule #1 is do nothing that could get you identified, even mis-identified as a 'spammer.' The best way to avoid this is to send e-mail sales letters only to prospects who have requested information from you or to customers who have given you permission. How often can you send e-mail follow-up to inquiries? There is no limit. As long as your e-mails are engaging and interesting, you can literally e-mail every day!—as many very successful Internet marketers do. The big challenges in using e-mail are not very different from regular mail: (a) getting your e-mail delivered, (b) getting it opened, (c) getting it read, (d) motivating the reader to action.

"Delivery means getting your e-mail past all the spam filters. Then, whether or not your e-mail is opened or not depends on the headline, i.e. the subject line, and the recipient's feelings about the name that appears on the 'from' line. In e-mail, the call to action that stimulates the most response is a clickable link to a Web site. Tip: Don't send prospects to your home page. Send them to a page that's a seamless continuation of the sales message in the e-mail. You can also deliver a complete sales letter in a PDF file."

If you recall earlier in this book, I spent a lot of time talking with you about "graphic enhancements" and illustrated sales letters. Platinum Member Yanik Silver, our resident Internet marketing advisor in my *No B.S. Marketing Letter*, is a master at the online illustrated and graphically enhanced sales letter. Some of his brief advice:

"Overall, I use graphic enhancements for online sales letters just as I do in print. There are only a few differences. For example, you don't want to underline, because underlining typically signals a link, so you can easily confuse people. Italics are hard to read. But I use a lot of boldface type, yellow highlighter marks, screened boxes, bullets, and color, as well as photos and illustrations. I even mark up letters as if I'd done it in handwriting!"

Resource!

You can get more of Ken McCarthy's advice in the Ultimate Sales Letter Course available free at *www.Ultimate-Sales-Letter.com*. You also can contact Ken directly and get information about the extraordinary seminars he occasionally conducts at *www.kenmccarthy.com*.

A good place to see one of Yanik's online sales letters loaded with graphic enhancements is at *www.InstantInternetProfits.com*.

A warning: A lot of the people selling Web site construction services, doing e-mail marketing, and so on are "techies" with little or no sales or marketing savvy or experience. They are at least as dangerous as graphic artists, if not more so. You need to carefully separate their valid advice on technical matters from their invalid advice on marketing matters. Contrary to what many of these tech types will insist, a strong sales letter is a strong sales letter is a strong sales letter regardless of the delivery medium being used. "What works" does *not* change significantly whether carving it on a rock, having it put on papyrus by a calligrapher, or posting it on a Web site.

Web Site Copywriting Tricks of the Trade

By Corey Rudl,
Founder,
Internet Marketing Center

We all know that well-written copy is one of the most highly effective methods of getting people's attention and attracting them to your product or service . . . but the importance of the shortest copy is often overlooked. A lot of people don't even realize that things like their navigation menus, links, and their offers *are* copy and require **careful consideration.**

Ironically, this kind of copy is one of the most valuable tools you have. Think about your . . .

- Banners
- Classified ads
- Navigation menus
- Links ("click here," "buy now")

This sort of copy is typically asking people to take some sort of action that is vital to your business: *visit* your Web site, *request* more info, *subscribe* to your newsletter, *click* through, *buy* the product . . . which is why it requires so much more attention than it tends to receive.

Of course it's more difficult to get your message across when you have limited space, but short copy is **the glue that holds your marketing campaign together.** And if every button on your menu, every ad, every link isn't as absolutely compelling and effective as it can be, you're not going to get the results you're hoping for, be it more sales, more subscriptions, more referrals, etc. . . .

So I'm going to show you **four rules of copywriting** that must be followed in even the shortest of copy to guarantee you always make the most profitable use of the little space you have.

COREY RUDL'S RULE #1
You MUST emphasize benefits, not features.

I know, I know, you've heard this one before. But I so often see copy—short and long—that *neglects to mention* how the features of a product or service will benefit customers, that I'm guessing a good number of you aren't sure what this really means. So let me clarify for you. . . .

- A **feature** is one of the components or functions of your product or service. For example, if your toothbrushes come packaged with glow-in-the-dark toothpaste, that's a feature—*not a benefit.*
- A **benefit** is something your product or service will do for your buyer to somehow offer a solution to a problem. So if your toothbrushes that come with glow-in-the-dark toothpaste make stubborn kids thrilled to brush their teeth before they go to bed, *then* you've got yourself a benefit!

Are you following me? An online real estate agent advertising "real-time mortgage calculations" is advertising a feature of her site; however, if she writes, "avoid wasting time haggling at the bank with my real-time mortgage calculator," then she's advertising a benefit.

Emphasizing benefits is the number one most overlooked rule of copywriting, and this lack of emphasis is one of the top reasons advertising falls flat. Short copy is no exception—and you don't need a lot of room to do it right.

Let's take a look at a short classified ad. If you posted an ad that read

Real estate on the Internet.
Plenty of listings.
Shop at your convenience.

... you probably wouldn't get the greatest response. The ad is brief and to the point, but it lacks clarity. First of all, what kind of property is being advertised? Are the listings for commercial buildings or family homes? What part of the world does the ad refer to? How many listings is "plenty"? How do we get to see these listings? And, most important, how does this service benefit me?

There is a vague reference to the benefit of "convenience" in this ad— but it's not really explained. Let's dress it up a bit:

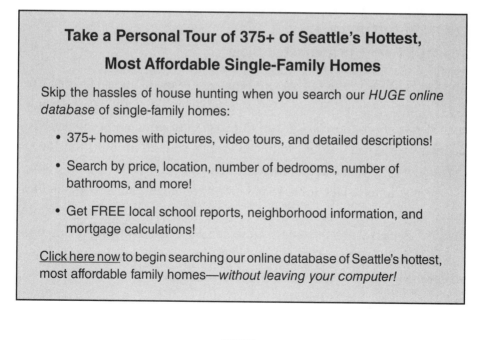

Take a Personal Tour of 375+ of Seattle's Hottest, Most Affordable Single-Family Homes

Skip the hassles of house hunting when you search our *HUGE online database* of single-family homes:

- 375+ homes with pictures, video tours, and detailed descriptions!

- Search by price, location, number of bedrooms, number of bathrooms, and more!

- Get FREE local school reports, neighborhood information, and mortgage calculations!

<u>Click here now</u> to begin searching our online database of Seattle's hottest, most affordable family homes—*without leaving your computer!*

This version expands on the benefit of convenience and details the different ways this convenience offers *solutions* to the house-hunter's problems. So the benefits we're clarifying for the reader are:

1. House hunting is a hassle and now you can avoid it.
2. Physically going to see 375 homes would be practically impossible, but you can easily do it online.
3. You can search the database by very specific criteria to effortlessly find exactly what you want.
4. Plus you'll get free reports that detail all the information you'll want to know about a new home and neighborhood that you wouldn't get even if you went there in person.

Also note that this ad targets a specific niche: single-family home buyers in the Seattle area. Targeting your advertising is the only way to get your benefits in front of your best potential customers, as we'll discover in the next Rule.

COREY RUDL'S RULE #2
You MUST write to a targeted audience.

The fact is, your product or service is just not going to appeal to everyone. And if you try to market it to everyone, you'll wind up with far fewer sales than if you choose a select group to direct your copy to. So once you've defined your target market, you need to turn your attention toward making sure your copy addresses them directly.

For example, let's look at pay-per-click advertising. Let's say you bid 17 cents per click in Overture.com for the key phrase "single-family homes." Because you pay every time someone clicks through this link, whether they purchase from you or not, you want to make sure that your ad **carefully targets your best potential customers.**

Given that you're targeting single-family home buyers in the Seattle area, you'd want to make sure your ad includes this vital piece of information. That way, you can be sure you won't waste money on people searching for single-family homes in San Diego!

And if you bid 41 cents per click for the key phrase "Seattle homes," you'd want to make sure to write an ad that clearly states that your site features single-family homes . . . so you don't waste your advertising dollars on condo-seekers or recreational property buyers.

By writing a separate ad for each of your keywords that carefully targets your market, you'll ensure that you **attract the most buyers for the least cost.**

Of course, if you're writing copy for banner ads, your approach will need to be a bit different. Whether you're:

1. Purchasing blocks of impressions (i.e., you pay a set dollar amount for your banner to be displayed 1,000 . . . 10,000 . . . etc. . . . times on other Web sites), or
2. Participating in a banner exchange (i.e., you're trading banner impressions with a network of other site owners).

You've paid for your advertising up front, so you'll want to do everything you can to attract viewers' attention and persuade them to click through to your site. And this means you'll want your ad copy to be a bit more general, **to ensure it attracts the highest number of click-throughs.**

The title of the above classified ad would make a great banner:

Take a Personal Tour of 375+ of Seattle's Hottest, Most Affordable Single-Family Homes! Click here now . . .

You're targeting your best potential customers! But you might also try testing banners with more general copy that reads something like this:

> **Search HUGE online database of 375+ Seattle dream homes and skip the house-hunting headaches! Click here now . . .**

The first ad is going to attract the most qualified audience—those who are looking for a single-family home in Seattle for a reasonable price. The second version, however, will **attract a slightly broader audience.** Still in Seattle and still looking for homes, this group is not necessarily looking for a single-family dwelling, and they're not necessarily worried about price. They're just checking out homes in the Seattle area and they're attracted by the size and convenience of the online database.

While the first ad may **generate a higher visitor-to-sale conversion rate** (the percentage of people clicking through who then sign up for the service) because it is more specific, the second ad will probably solicit more click-throughs in total, because it has a more general appeal. You'd have to test to see which version would pull the most sign-ups altogether.

COREY RUDL'S RULE #3
You MUST include a call to action.

Okay, easy enough. BUY NOW! There's a call to action.

But hold on a minute. If it were that simple, everyone marketing online would be rich, and every online shopper would have to move into a bigger home to accommodate all that happily purchased stuff.

There are two very important things that you must include in your call to action:

1. You must determine *exactly what* action you want people to take.
2. You must provide a reason *why* people should take that action.

Isn't *buy now* exactly the action you want? Not necessarily. Think about what exactly it is that you are trying to do. Are you trying to generate leads? Do you want people to sign up for your free newsletter? Are you trying to attract a specific audience and hoping to convert as many of those people as possible into sales?

It is important to understand that *all* copy, if possible, should contain a call to action that clearly identifies what action is desired. I can't emphasize this enough.

Think about the buttons on your site menu. Each one is a call to action—and they are all very important! If they're not as direct as possible, not telling visitors *specifically* what to do, they will be useless.

For example, if you have a button that is labeled "sales," you are doing nothing but confusing your visitors, leaving them guessing whether you are referring to *product* sales (i.e., online ordering), products that are *on* sale (i.e., specials or discounts), or maybe the opportunity to *sell* your product (i.e., merchandising opportunities). But your visitors won't guess for long—why would they bother? They'll just leave your site.

If you change the button copy from "sales" to "order online," you are now asking viewers to take an action—to order your product. This clarifies the purpose of the button and tells the viewer what to do to get your product. Another example: Instead of writing "E-mail," you could ask your viewers to "Contact Us"—again, you're asking your visitors to take a specific action!

Of course, you will not always be able to include a call to action in every button; you won't always have the space. Your best bet in this case is to **be as clear as possible.**

For example, it would be difficult to include a call to action in a button of your navigation menu that leads to your newsletter back issues. There would not be room to say "click here now to read our newsletter back issues." So in this case, you'd just want to make sure that your copy is clear. Label the button "Newsletter Back Issues" instead of "More" or "Old Stuff."

Now let's think about your links. Suppose "buy now" is the action you want. You have to give people a *reason why* they should buy. Huge, garishly colored words on a screen won't do the trick; added benefits will.

In your links, you have a little more room to move. The call to action should remain the central focus of the link, but pack in as many benefits as possible around it. Something like this will win out every time over "Buy Now":

> **Click here now** to claim your *"Golfer's Guide to the Green"* and instantly receive the downloadable video that features up-close-and-personal interviews with Pro Golfers who reveal their hottest golfing secrets, guaranteed to improve your game in 2 weeks or your money back!

COREY RUDL'S RULE #4
You MUST pay attention to layout.

Making the most of your layout is especially important when you're writing short copy. The right blend of emphasis and information is the best way to attract viewers. Don't underestimate the effectiveness of bolding, italics, underlining, color, and white space.

But don't overdo it either!

For example, **an offer to subscribe to a newsletter must be brief, compelling, and effective.** It will not be the main feature of your Web page or anyone else's, so it must be attractive enough to grab the attention of a distracted reader. But it also needs to remain readable and informative, without a gross misuse of formatting tricks.

If your ad has too much going on it, it will look unattractive, unappealing, and unprofessional—and the clutter will detract from the meaning of your message.

On the other hand, too little emphasis leaves you in danger of never catching anyone's eye. If your ad is totally boring, no one will ever even see it—and if they somehow do, they probably won't look at it long enough to find out what it's about.

So let's try to find a happy medium, emphasizing without crowding. Take a look at the ad for the Potato Farmers newsletter.

Subscribe to our FREE "Potato Farmers" Newsletter

Subscribe today to the FREE "Potato Farmers" newsletter and on the first Tuesday of each month you'll receive tips and strategies from industry leaders who'll reveal:

- Secrets for selling your crops for the highest profits!
- Tricks for cutting down the time you spend in the field!
- Cost-effective strategies for tripling your crop yield!
- Plus much, much more!

Each issue contains tons of easy-to-implement techniques, guaranteed to *reduce your expenses while dramatically increasing your annual income!*

Click Here Now To Subscribe!

Catchy, effective, and professional in appearance, the newsletter ad draws your attention and doesn't distract you from the information it contains once you're there.

The ad is clearly laid out and easy to read. In the actual newsletter, the title is underlined and in blue, as is the link. This is the standard way to handle links, and it lets the viewers know they can link to the sign-up page from either place. **Giving readers two chances to link through to your sign-up will always work better than one.** (And never have any blue, underlined text that is not a link!)

I've used only subtle formatting tricks to provide emphasis while keeping the ad visually appealing. The title of the newsletter is in quotation marks to give it additional emphasis. The main features of the newsletter—what you'll learn from the experts—are emphasized by bullet points and a nice amount of white space. And the main benefits of the newsletter—*reduce your expenses while dramatically increasing your annual income*—are italicized and strategically placed right before the call to action.

Because the **call to action** comes at the end of the ad, it is supported by all that came before it. And because it is the last bit of text and will appear in blue, the viewer's eye is effectively drawn through the ad after being attracted by the title.

Of course, some of the formatting techniques discussed here are available only to people who format their ads in HTML. Obviously, you have more options in HTML and can do pretty much whatever you like. But in text format, you don't have the choice of adding color, bold, italics, and so on. You *do*, however, have the ability to use characters, spacing, capitalization, and indentation for effect.

So if we had to format the Potato Farmers newsletter ad in text, it might look like the one in the accompanying box.

"FREE Subscription to 'Potato Farmers' Newsletter'"
Subscribe today and on the first Tuesday of each month you'll receive tips and strategies from INDUSTRY LEADERS who'll reveal . . .

1. Secrets for selling your crops for the HIGHEST PROFITS!
2. Tricks for cutting down the time you spend in the field!
3. Cost-effective strategies for TRIPLING YOUR CROP YIELD!
4. Plus much, much more!

Each issue contains tons of easy-to-implement techniques, guaranteed to REDUCE YOUR EXPENSES while dramatically INCREASING YOUR ANNUAL INCOME!
Visit http://www.PotatoFarmers.com to subscribe!

Because we don't have the option of hyperlinking the text, which effectively highlights it in blue, I've moved the capitalized "FREE" to the beginning of the title to attract attention. I've also enclosed the headline in quotation marks for emphasis, and put the newsletter title in single quotes (which should always be used inside double quotes).

I've capitalized the benefits that were italicized in the HTML version along with a few more benefits to **make the ad as eye-catching as possible.** The general rule in text is to capitalize whatever you would have bolded or italicized in HTML, but be careful—caps are difficult to read if used excessively.

Final Thoughts

So now that you know the secrets of fitting high-impact copy into small spaces, I'll let you in on another little secret . . . there's a lot more to learn!

In fact, this article itself has been an exercise in fitting tons of information into a relatively small space. Writing sales copy, designing banner ads, writing powerful classified ads, putting together an effective newsletter subscription offer . . . these are all topics that I've devoted *entire lessons* (i.e., hundreds of pages) to in my Insider Secrets course.

However, now that you have some of the basics under your belt, you should be able to start making dramatic improvements to your short copy . . . improvements that will attract a much bigger response and increased sales! If all your copy is written with the rules of benefits, audience, call to action, and layout in mind, you simply can't lose.

And remember: No amount of copy is so small that it can be overlooked. Every link, button, banner, and classified ad is either making or breaking your marketing campaign as we speak!

Resource!

The Internet Marketing Center's complete course, The Insider Secrets To Marketing Your Business On The Internet, contains more than 1,000 pages, including step-by-step, illustrated instructions to build, automate, and create traffic for your Web site. It also teaches you about advanced marketing and how to turn an existing Web site into a "money machine." Details about the course are at *www.mar-ketingtips.com/kennedy*. Also, one of the lessons in the 12-Week Ultimate Marketing Plan Course delivered by e-mail has been prepared by The Internet Marketing Center. You can enroll in the course free at *www.UltimateMarketingPlan.com*.

FREE RESOURCES
TO HELP YOU PROFIT FROM THIS BOOK!

TWO TICKETS ($995.00 Value Each If Purchased) TO THE ULTI-MATE 1-DAY MARKETING & WEALTH CREATION TRAINING CONFERENCE featuring Dan Kennedy, Zig Ziglar, Bill Glazer (on "Outrageous Advertising"), Paul Hartunian (on "Free Publicity"), Ron LeGrand (on "Multiple Income Streams"), Yanik Silver (on "Internet Opportunities") and other outstanding speakers and experts. This is a limited time offer. If you are purchasing the book after the Conference (late 2006), you will receive an alternate gift. Complete details and FREE REGISTRATION at: www.Ultimate-Sales-Letter.com

ENTER THE NATIONAL SALES LETTER / MARKETING PLAN CONTEST and compete for a new Ford Mustang and other exciting prizes, and have your sales letter/marketing plan evaluated by a panel of expert judges. If you are purchasing this book after the Contest is com-pleted, you will be offered a different opportunity to compete for other prizes or an alternate gift. Complete details and FREE ENTRY at www. NationalSalesLetterContest.com

FREE SALES LETTER WRITING E-MAIL COURSE, a multi-week extension of this book, complete with examples and useful tools. And, a FREE TELESEMINAR (or replay recording). Register at www.Ultimate-Sales-Letter.com (Anything else referenced throughout this book can also be accessed via this Web site.)

<u>Special Free Gift From The Author</u>

Copy this page and FAX to 410-727-0978
Or go to www.Ultimate-Sales-Letter.com

**FREE: Test Drive Three Months of Dan Kennedy's
Gold Inner Circle Membership**

Includes:

1. Three months of the *No B.S. Marketing Letter*
2. Three months of Exclusive Audio Interviews
3. Three months, Marketing Gold Hotsheet
4. Gold Members' Restricted Access Archives Web Site
5. Million Dollar Resource Directory

There is a one-time charge of $5.95 to cover postage for ALL three months of the FREE Gold Membership, and you have no obligation to continue at the lowest Gold Member price of $39.97 per month ($49.97 outside North America). In fact, should you continue with Membership, you may later cancel at any time.

Name _____ Business Name _____

Address _____ __ Business __ Home

City, State, Zip _____

E-Mail _____

FAX _____ Phone _____

__ AmericanExpress   __ VISA   __ MasterCard

Card# _____ Exp Date _____

Signature _____ Date _____

Providing this information constitutes your permission for Glazer-Kennedy Inner Circle LLC to contact you regarding related information via above listed means.

OTHER INFORMATION FROM THE AUTHOR

SPEAKING ENGAGEMENTS, CONSULTING OR COPYWRITING ASSIGNMENTS, information at www.dankennedy.com. Direct contact to Mr. Kennedy's office, fax 602-269-3113.

Other Books By The Author

The Ultimate Marketing Plan (Adams Media)
No B.S. Sales Success (Entrepreneur Press)
No B.S. Business Success (Entrepreneur Press)
No B.S. Time Management For Entrepreneurs (Entrepreneur Press)
No B.S. Wealth Attraction For Entrepreneurs (Entrepreneur Press)
No B.S. Direct Marketing For Non-Direct Marketing Businesses
   (Entrepreneur Press)
Make Millions With Your Ideas (Plume)

Catalog Of Dan Kennedy Resources: www.Ultimate-Sales-Letter.com

Other Web Sites Of Interest

www.nobsbooks.com
www.psycho-cybernetics.com
www.renegademillionaire.com

Resource Directory

In this Resource Directory, you will first find people mentioned in the book whom you might want to contact, listed in order of first appearance, by page number. You will also find a second section, with contacts and vendors in category groups. A much more extensive, frequently updated Resource Directory is provided to all Glazer-Kennedy Inner Circle Members who receive my *No B.S. Marketing Letter*. You can arrange a free three-month membership with no obligation at *www.Ultimate-Sales-Letter.com*.

Darin Garman, Real Estate Marketing Systems,   page 7
Craig Forte,   pages 21–22
Craig Proctor,   page 22
Tracy Tolleson, Tolleson Mortgage Publications, Inc.,   page 22
Jerry Jones, Jerry Jones Direct,   page 26
Ron LeGrand, Global Publishing Inc.,   page 27
Pamela Yellen, Prospecting & Marketing Institute,   page 29
Rory Fatt, Restaurant Marketing Systems, Inc.,   page 41
Bill Glazer, President, Glazer-Kennedy Inner Circle, Inc.,   page 43
Dr. Barry Lycka,   page 53
Mitch Carson, CEO, Impact Products,   page 56

Dr. Chris Brady,   page 59

Craig Dickhout, Think Ink,   page 37

Yanik Silver,   page 72

Ted Thomas, Trevor & Jones Marketing,   page 131

Scott Tucker, Tucker Family Financial,   page 132

Corey Rudl, CEO, Internet Marketing Center,   page 191

Ken McCarthy, Amacord,   page 192

Platinum Members

Dr. Chris Brady
The Brady Group
3940 Timber Lane
Colorado Springs, CO 80908
Phone: 719-495-3168
Fax: 719-466-9119

Craig Brockie
Defining Presence Marketing Group
2707–83 Garry Street
Winnipeg, Manitoba R3C 4J9
CANADA
Phone: 204-982-0011
Fax: 604-648-9673

Rory Fatt
Restaurant Marketing Systems
7198 Vantage Way
#104
Delta, BC V4G 1K7
CANADA
Phone: 604-940-6900
Fax: 604-940-6902
Web site: *www.roryfatt.com*

Jay M. Geier
Scheduling Institute
1875 Old Alabama
Suite #845
Roswell, GA 30076
Phone: 770-518-7575
Fax: 770-518-7577

Bill Glazer
Glazer-Kennedy Inner Circle, Inc. &
BGS Marketing
407 West Pennsylvania Avenue
Towson, MD 21204
Phone: 410-825-8600
Fax: 410-825-3301
Web site: *www.bgsmarketing.com*

Bill & Steve Harrison
Bradley Communications Corp.
135 E. Plumstead Avenue
Lansdowne, PA 19050
Phone: 610-259-1070
Fax: 610-259-5032

Reed Hoisington
Reed Hoisington Pub. Inc.
2413 Morganton Road
Fayetteville, NC 28303
Phone: 910-484-4519
Fax: 910-485-3524

Chauncey Hutter Jr.
Real Tax Business Success
504 Old Lynchburg Road
Suite #2
Charlottesville, VA 22903
Phone: 434-220-4705
Fax: 434-220-4706

Ron Ipach
CinRon Marketing Group
7908 Cincinnati-Dayton Road
Suite O
West Chester, OH 45069
Phone: 513-779-3660
Fax: 513-779-4990

Alan Jacques & D.J. Richoux
Business Breakthrough Tech.
4058 Wellington Street
Port Coquitlam, BC V3B 3Z7
CANADA
Phone: 604-552-9431
Fax: 604-552-9429

Jerry Jones
Jerry Jones Direct
1020 Shipping Street NE
Salem, OR 97303
Phone: 503-371-1390
Fax: 503-371-1299

Michael Kimble
Group M Marketing Inc.
9433 Bee Cave Road
Bldg. 2, Suite 110
Austin, TX 78733
Phone: 512-263-2299
Fax: 512-263-9898

Ron LeGrand
Global Publishing Inc.
9799 Old St. Augustine Road
Jacksonville, FL 32257
Phone: 888-840-8389 / 904-262-0491
Fax: 888-840-8385 / 904-421-0182
Web site: *www.RonLeGrand.com*

John Paul Mendocha
Speed Selling
11800 Della Lane
Grand Terrace, CA 92313
Phone: 909-783-4400
Fax: 909-370-1170

Corey Rudl / Internet Marketing Center
#400–1155 W. Pender Street
Vancouver, BC V6E 2P4
CANADA
Phone: 604-730-2833
Fax: 604-638-6015

Yanik Silver
Surefire Marketing Inc.
10832 Brewer House Road
N. Bethesda, MD 20852
Phone: 301-770-0423
Fax: 301-770-1096

Platinum Members (concluded)

Ted Thomas
Trevor & Jones Marketing
3525 N. Courtney
Suite B
Merritt Island, FL 32953
Phone: 321-449-9940
Fax: 321-449-9938

Dr. Robert Willis
The Coaching Program
5908 E. 106th Street
Tulsa, OK 74137
Phone: 918-688-8848
Fax: 918-298-7943

Resources by Category

DIRECT MAIL

Mitch Carson
Impact Products
5331 Derry Avenue
Suite J
Agoura Hills, CA 91301
Phone: 888-215-4758
Fax: 818-707-1777
Web site: *www.impactproducts.net*

Craig Dickhout
Think Inc.
19891 Beach Boulevard
Suite #35
Huntington Beach, CA 92648
Phone: 714-374-7080
Fax: 714-374-7071
E-mail: *sales@thinkinkmarketing.com*

INTERNET MARKETING

Ken McCarthy
Amacord
Web site: *www.AMACORD.com*

Corey Rudl / Internet Marketing Center
#400–1155 W. Pender Street
Vancouver, BC V6E 2P4
CANADA
Phone: 604-730-2833
Fax: 604-638-6015

Yanik Silver
Surefire Marketing Inc.
10832 Brewer House Road
N. Bethesda, MD 20852
Phone: 301-770-0423
Fax: 301-770-1096

SPECIALIZED MARKETING ADVISORS

For Chiropractors, Cosmetic Surgeons, Dentists, Cosmetic Dentists, and Other Professional Practices

Dr. Chris Brady
The Brady Group
3940 Timber Lane
Colorado Springs, CO 80908
Phone: 719-495-3168
Fax: 719-466-9119

Dr. Barry Lycka
780–10665 Jasper Avenue
Edmonton, AB T5J 3S9
CANADA
Phone: 780-425-1212
Fax: 780-425-1217
Web site: *www.cosmeticsx.com*

Jerry Jones
Jerry Jones Direct
1020 Shipping Street NE
Salem, OR 97303
Phone: 503-371-1390
Fax: 503-371-1299

Dr. Robert Willis
The Coaching Program
5908 E. 106th Street
Tulsa, OK 74137
Phone: 918-688-8848
Fax: 918-298-7943

For Direct Marketing for All Businesses

Dan Kennedy
5818 N. 7th Street, Suite #103
Phoenix, AZ 85014
Phone: 602-997-7707
Fax: 602-269-3113
Web site: *www.dankennedy.com*

Ted Thomas
Trevor & Jones Marketing
3525 N. Courtney
Suite B
Merritt Island, FL 32953
Phone: 321-449-9940
Fax: 321-449-9938

Michael Kimble
Group M Marketing Inc.
9433 Bee Cave Road
Bldg. 2, Suite 110
Austin, TX 78733
Phone: 512-263-2299
Fax: 512-263-9898

For Restaurants

Rory Fatt
Restaurant Marketing Systems
7198 Vantage Way
#104
Delta, BC V4G 1K7
CANADA
Phone: 604-940-6900
Fax: 604-940-6902
Web site: *www.roryfatt.com*

For Mortgage Brokers and Lenders

Reed Hoisington
Reed Hoisington Pub. Inc.
2413 Morganton Road
Fayetteville, NC 28303
Phone: 910-484-4519
Fax: 910-485-3524

Scott Tucker
2154 W. Roscoe Street
Chicago, IL 60618
Free Report, Coaching Program:
800-894-1493
Fax: 773-327-2842
Web site: *www.*
mortgagemarketinggenius.com

Tracy Tolleson
Tolleson Mortgage Publications Inc.
5818 N. 7th Street, Suite #103
Phoenix, AZ 85014
Phone: 602-265-1922
Fax: 602-269-3113

For Real Estate Agents

Craig Forte
Service For Life
Fax: 520-546-1359

Craig Proctor
Craig Proctor Productions
1111 Stellar Drive
Suite #12
Newmarket, ON L3Y 7B8
CANADA
Phone: 905-640-0449
Fax: 905-640-0448
Web site:
www.QuantumLeapSystems.com

For Real Estate Investors

Darin Garman
Real Estate Marketing Systems
3045 Winston Circle
Marion, IA 52302
Phone: 319-350-5378
Fax: 319-373-5535
Web site: *www.commercial-investments.com*

Alan Jacques & D.J. Richoux
Business Breakthrough Technologies
4058 Wellington Street
Port Coquitlam, BC V3B 3Z7
CANADA
Phone: 604-552-9431
Fax: 604-552-9429

Ron LeGrand
Global Publishing Inc.
9799 Old St. Augustine Road
Jacksonville, FL 32257
Phone: 888-840-8389 / 904-262-0491
Fax: 888-840-8385 / 904-421-0182
Web site: *www.RonLeGrand.com*

Ted Thomas
Trevor & Jones Marketing
3525 N. Courtney
Suite B
Merritt Island, FL 32953
Phone: 321-449-9940
Fax: 321-449-9938

For Retail Businesses

Kevin Fayle
Profit Advantage Enterprise Inc.
3621 Wildflower Circle
Syracuse, NY 13215
Phone: 800-836-3904
Fax: 315-492-0585

Bill Glazer
Glazer-Kennedy Inner Circle, Inc.
& BGS Marketing
407 West Pennsylvania Avenue
Towson, MD 21204
Phone: 410-825-8600
Fax: 410-825-3301
Web site: *www.bgsmarketing.com*

For Sales Professionals

John Paul Mendocha
Speed Selling
11800 Della Lane
Grand Terrace, CA 92313
Phone: 909-783-4400
Fax: 909-370-1170

For Insurance and Financial Services

Pamela Yellen
Prospecting & Marketing Institute
Fax: 505-466-2167

FREE

ENTER
THE NATIONAL ULTIMATE SALES LETTER
CONTEST!

Expert judges will assess your best sales letter and the marketing plan it is part of, and you may win a Ford Mustang, other great prizes, tele-seminars—and you will be motivated to put everything in this book to practical use! The author and the publisher are eager to see you use the strategies in this book, not just read about them!

REGISTER TO PARTICIPATE FREE, NOW

at

www.NationalSalesLetterContest.com.

No purchase necessary to participate. If you read this book in a library, someone's office, at your company, it does not matter. Anyone can participate.

Index

A

address designations, 37, 164–65
advertorials, 68–70
agitation copy, 78–79
American Speaker, 69
analytical prospects, 103–05
application process, for
    prospective customers, 88–89
attention grabbers
    advertorials, 68–70
    celebrities, 53–54
    color, 57
    grabbers, 55–57
    graphics, 129–39, 152, 193
    headlines, 47–53, 109, 111
    involvement devices, 57
    photographs, 58
    testimonials, 58
    valuable information, 46–47
author alterations (AAs), 160
auto-responders, 191–92
availability, limited, 87, 120

B

bandwagon effect, 88
believability, 58
benefits
    emphasizing, 196–98
    listing, 28–30

Brady, Chris, 59, 212, 215
brand recognition, 181
Brockie, Craig, 212
bulk mail, 36
bulk selling, 73
business, understanding of, 3, 5
business owners, tips for mailing
    to, 54–55
buyer's remorse, 176–80

C

calls to action, 200–202
Carson, Mitch, 56–57, 214
celebrities, 53–54, 165
checklists, 128
cold calls, 168
color, 57. *See also* graphic
    enhancements
comparisons
    apple to oranges, 71–72
    to other sales letters, 146
    winners and losers, 84–85
contests, 125
cooling-off period, 155
copywriting techniques
    appeal to senses, 112–13
    calls to action, 200–202
    conversational language,
        102–03
    demonstrate ROI, 89–90